EVALUATION OF CAPACITY TO CONSENT TO TREATMENT AND RESEARCH

D1537185

BEST PRACTICES IN FORENSIC MENTAL HEALTH ASSESSMENT

Series Editors

Thomas Grisso, Alan M. Goldstein, and Kirk Heilbrun

Series Advisory Board

Paul Appelbaum, Richard Bonnie, and John Monahan

Titles in the Series

Foundations of Forensic Mental Health Assessment, *Kirk Heilbrun, Thomas Grisso, and Alan M. Goldstein*

Criminal Titles

Evaluation of Competence to Stand Trial, *Patricia A. Zapf and Ronald Roesch*

Evaluation of Criminal Responsibility, *Ira K. Packer*

Evaluation of Capacity to Confess, *Alan M. Goldstein and Naomi Goldstein*

Evaluation of Sexually Violent Predators, *Philip H. Witt and Mary Alice Conroy*

Evaluation for Risk of Violence in Adults, *Kirk Heilbrun*

Jury Selection, *Margaret Bull Kovera and Brian L. Cutler*

Evaluation for Capital Sentencing, *Mark D. Cunningham*

Eyewitness Identification, *Brian L. Cutler and Margaret Bull Kovera*

Civil Titles

Evaluation of Capacity to Consent to Treatment and Research, *Scott Y. H. Kim*

Evaluation for Guardianship, *Eric Y. Drogin and Curtis L. Barrett*

Evaluation for Personal Injury Claims, *Andrew W. Kane and Joel Dvoskin*

Evaluation for Civil Commitment, *Debra Pinals and Douglas Mossman*

Evaluation for Harassment and Discrimination Claims, *William Foote and Jane Goodman-Delahunty*

Evaluation of Workplace Disability, *Lisa D. Piechowski*

Juvenile and Family Titles

Evaluation for Child Custody, *Geri S.W. Fuhrmann*

Evaluation of Juveniles' Competence to Stand Trial, *Ivan Kruh and Thomas Grisso*

Evaluation for Risk of Violence in Juveniles, *Robert Hoge and D.A. Andrews*

Evaluation for Child Protection, *Karen S. Budd, Jennifer Clark, Mary Connell, and Kathryn Kuehnle*

Evaluation for Disposition and Transfer of Juvenile Offenders, *Randall T. Salekin*

EVALUATION OF CAPACITY TO CONSENT TO TREATMENT AND RESEARCH

SCOTT Y. H. KIM

OXFORD
UNIVERSITY PRESS

2010

Oxford University Press, Inc., publishes works that further
Oxford University's objective of excellence
in research, scholarship, and education.

Oxford   New York
Auckland   Cape Town   Dar es Salaam   Hong Kong   Karachi
Kuala Lumpur   Madrid   Melbourne   Mexico City   Nairobi
New Delhi   Shanghai   Taipei   Toronto

With offices in
Argentina   Austria   Brazil   Chile   Czech Republic   France   Greece
Guatemala   Hungary   Italy   Japan   Poland   Portugal   Singapore
South Korea   Switzerland   Thailand   Turkey   Ukraine   Vietnam

Copyright © 2010 by Oxford University Press, Inc.

Published by Oxford University Press, Inc.
198 Madison Avenue, New York, New York 10016

www.oup.com

Oxford is a registered trademark of Oxford University Press

Library of Congress Cataloging-in-Publication Data
Kim, Scott Y. H.
Evaluation of capacity to consent to treatment and research / Scott Y.H. Kim.
p. ; cm. — (Best practices in forensic mental health assessment)
Includes bibliographical references and index.
Summary: "This book addresses the assessment of an individual's competency to
consent to medical treatment and using the template will look at the history and
importance of this process, the legal standards and the procedure for applying this
assessment in court. Established empirical foundations from the behavioral, social,
and medical sciences are then presented. Finally, the book provides a detailed
'how-to' for practitioners, including information on data collection, interpretation,
report writing and expert testimony"—Provided by publisher.
ISBN 978-0-19-532295-8
1. Forensic psychiatry.   2. Mental status examination.   3. Informed consent
(Medical law)   I. Title.   II. Series: Best practices in forensic mental health assessment.
[DNLM: 1. Forensic Psychiatry—methods—Great Britain.   2. Forensic Psychiatry—
methods—United States.   3. Informed Consent—psychology—Great Britain.
4. Informed Consent—psychology—United States.   5. Mental Competency—
psychology—Great Britain.   6. Mental Competency—psychology—United States.
7. Personality Assessment—Great Britain.   8. Personality Assessment—United States.
W 740 K49e 2010]
RA1151.K56 2010
614'.1—dc22

2009040523

ISBN 978-0-19-532295-8

9 8 7 6 5 4 3 2 1

Printed in the United States of America
on acid-free paper

About Best Practices in Forensic Mental Health Assessment

The recent growth of the fields of forensic psychology and forensic psychiatry has created a need for this book series describing best practices in forensic mental health assessment (FMHA). Currently, forensic evaluations are conducted by mental health professionals for a variety of criminal, civil, and juvenile legal questions. The research foundation supporting these assessments has become broader and deeper in recent decades. Consensus has become clearer on the recognition of essential requirements for ethical and professional conduct. In the larger context of the current emphasis on "empirically supported" assessment and intervention in psychiatry and psychology, the specialization of FMHA has advanced sufficiently to justify a series devoted to best practices. Although this series focuses mainly on evaluations conducted by psychologists and psychiatrists, the fundamentals and principles offered also apply to evaluations conducted by clinical social workers, psychiatric nurses, and other mental health professionals.

This series describes "best practice" as empirically supported (when the relevant research is available), legally relevant, and consistent with applicable ethical and professional standards. Authors of the books in this series identify the approaches that seem best, while incorporating what is practical and acknowledging that best practice represents a goal to which the forensic clinician should aspire, rather than a standard that can always be met. The American Academy of Forensic Psychology assisted the editors in enlisting the consultation of board-certified forensic psychologists specialized in each topic area. Board-certified forensic psychiatrists were also consultants on many of the volumes. Their comments on the manuscripts helped to ensure that the methods described in these volumes represent a generally accepted view of best practice.

The series' authors were selected for their specific expertise in a particular area. At the broadest level, however, certain general principles apply to all types of forensic evaluations. Rather than repeat those fundamental principles in every volume, the series offers them in the first volume, Foundations of Forensic Mental Health Assessment. Reading the first book, followed by a specific topical book, will provide the reader both the general principles that the specific topic shares with all forensic evaluations and those that are particular to the specific assessment question.

The specific topics of the 19 books were selected by the series editors as the most important and oft-considered areas of forensic assessment conducted by mental health professionals and behavioral scientists. Each of the 19 topical books is organized according to a common template. The authors address the applicable legal context, forensic mental health concepts, and empirical foundations and limits in the "Foundation" part of the book. They then describe preparation for the evaluation, data collection, data interpretation, and report writing and testimony in the "Application" part of the book. This creates a fairly uniform approach to considering these areas across different topics. All authors in this series have attempted to be as concise as possible in addressing best practice in their area. In addition, topical volumes feature elements to make them user friendly in actual practice. These elements include boxes that highlight especially important information, relevant case law, best-practice guidelines, and cautions against common pitfalls. A glossary of key terms is also provided in each volume.

We hope the series will be useful for different groups of individuals. Practicing forensic clinicians will find succinct, current information relevant to their practice. Those who are in training to specialize in forensic mental health assessment (whether in formal training or in the process of respecialization) should find helpful the combination of broadly applicable considerations presented in the first volume together with the more specific aspects of other volumes in the series. Those who teach and supervise trainees can offer these volumes as a guide for practices to which the trainee can aspire. Researchers and scholars interested in FMHA best practice may find researchable ideas, particularly on topics that have received insufficient research attention to date. Judges and attorneys with questions about FMHA best practice will find these books relevant and concise. Clinical and forensic administrators who run agencies, court clinics, and hospitals in which litigants are assessed may also use some of the books in this series to establish expectancies for evaluations performed by professionals in their agencies.

We also anticipate that the 19 specific books in this series will serve as reference works that help courts and attorneys evaluate the quality of forensic mental health professionals' evaluations. A word of caution is in order, however. These volumes focus on best practice, not what is minimally acceptable legally or ethically. Courts involved in malpractice litigation, or ethics committees or licensure boards considering complaints, should not expect that materials describing best practice easily or necessarily translate into the minimally acceptable professional conduct that is typically at issue in such proceedings.

The present volume addresses best practices in conducting evaluations of patients' competence to consent to treatment or to research participation. Modern law and ethics require that patients must be fully informed of their treatment options, and that treatment cannot proceed without their competent consent. In this context, questions of competence are often raised when a patient appears to have dubious capacities for deciding on a treatment, and when the treatment itself is considered to have important consequences, sometimes involving life-saving intervention.

Because of the ethical and legal requirements for consent to treatment, the question of competence to consent arises daily in the ordinary practice of medicine, psychiatry, and psychology. Unlike evaluations addressed in most other volumes in this series, evaluations for competence to consent to treatment typically are not ordered by a court. They are evaluations that must be done, often informally but sometimes formally, with every patient for whom a treatment is being recommended. Typically this "evaluation" is no more than an awareness on the doctor's part that the patient is responding "normally" and without unusual difficulty. In this sense, most assessments of patients' competence are done by physicians, psychiatrists, and psychologists who do not consider themselves to be "forensic" specialists, yet are responsible for assuring that their patient is making an informed and competent choice.

For forensically specialized clinicians who work in clinical settings, competence to consent to evaluations often is requested in difficult cases, where the clinical and legal reasoning involved may need more sophisticated attention than is available to the nonforensic clinician. In addition, they should be able to guide their nonforensic colleagues to use best practices in evaluating their patients' capacities. In summary, understanding and performing evaluations for competence to consent to treatment is of considerable importance especially for forensic clinicians who work in medical settings. This volume provides the concepts and methods that currently represent best practices in the conduct of evaluations for competence to consent to treatment and to research participation.

Thomas Grisso
Alan M. Goldstein
Kirk Heilbrun

Acknowledgments

I thank Paul Appelbaum, M.D. for helpful comments on an earlier draft and Thomas Grisso, Ph.D. for his judicious editing. This book moreover owes a great deal to their pioneering work in the field of capacity assessment. I also thank Sandra Moing for assistance with the manuscript.

Contents

FOUNDATION

The Legal Context | 1

Purpose and History of Capacity to Consent to Treatment

Patients provide valid *informed consent* to a treatment or a diagnostic procedure if they have sufficient capacity, have been given appropriate information, and give consent freely without coercion or undue influence. When a patient's capacity for treatment consent is in doubt, a clinician must determine whether the patient indeed has the capacity. It is a common reason behind requests for psychiatric consultations in a general hospital (Appelbaum, 2007). Furthermore, a significant proportion of medical inpatients have impaired abilities relevant to providing informed consent, often unrecognized by the treating team (Raymont et al., 2004).

The clinician's determination of a patient's capacity to provide informed consent can have serious consequences. Consider a patient who is refusing a life-sustaining treatment. If the patient is capable but is mistakenly determined to lack capacity, that person's right to self-determination may well be violated. In a society that places a very high value on autonomy, this is a serious breach of a fundamental right. Indeed, a competent patient's right to refuse treatment—even life-sustaining treatment—is, as one legal scholar puts it, "about as close to absolute as anything ever gets in law" (Meisel, 1998, p. 241).

But if the patient is actually incapable of making such a decision and is allowed to make his own decision, then we risk abandoning the patient to his "rights." In a life or death situation, this would be an irreversible failure to protect a particularly vulnerable patient—someone who has lost the very faculty of self-determination. Failure to protect such patients, especially by health care professionals whose societally sanctioned role is to promote the health and well-being of patients, would be a grave error.

A patient's consent capacity is an ethically and legally required element of informed consent. In most medical treatment situations, the courts are not involved and the clinician's judgment carries the day (Appelbaum, 2007). Yet the legal criteria for competence that are meant to guide clinician evaluators vary by jurisdiction, and they are usually broadly worded and provide little concrete guidance. There are no widely accepted curricula for teaching clinicians how to evaluate treatment consent capacity. Although there is an increasing amount of research on the topic, the field of capacity research remains small.

The upshot is that our society—by intention, historical accident, and practical necessity—places a tremendous amount of trust in the interpretations and judgments of clinicians in the health care setting in determining a patient's capacity to provide informed consent. (An exceptional setting is the inpatient psychiatric unit or hospital, where cases can more often end up in courts because of special laws regarding psychiatric treatment of incompetent patients. See chapter 7.) Although the current practice is guided, and certainly delimited, by law, much of that practice has arisen from ground up, from the practical necessity of clinicians being placed in positions of making capacity determinations. Within the broad guidelines of the law, experts in the field over the past 30 years have developed a set of interpretations and practices that have achieved some consensus. This book largely draws on and, it is hoped, further refines that development.

In this chapter, we begin with the legal and social context of consent capacity assessments—its contours and history. Because the assessment of consent capacity is highly context sensitive and requires considerable judgment, the evaluator must thoroughly grasp the basic legal and ethical principles to guide such an assessment. And this in turn requires an understanding of the history and purpose of the doctrine of informed consent.

Legal History of Informed Consent

The legal doctrine of informed consent is about 30–50 years old, as most scholars point to a series of cases from the mid-1950s through 1970s as the origins of the modern doctrine (Berg, Appelbaum, Lidz, & Parker, 2001; Faden & Beauchamp, 1986; Garrison & Schneider, 2003). In fact, the American Medical Association did not publish an official policy on informed consent until 1981 (Faden & Beauchamp, 1986). This does not mean that doctors forcibly imposed operations (the literature and law on consent is often a story about surgical treatments) on patients without their knowledge and consent prior to that period. The practice of obtaining the consent of the patient for surgical procedures is as old as medicine. Often cited is *Slater v. Baker and Stapleton* (1767), an English case in which the court's opinion unambiguously indicates that the norm at the time was that the patient had to give consent to a surgical procedure. There are also well-documented cases in the medical literature from the first half of the 19th century in which patients died after their refusal of recommended treatments were honored by their physicians (after being provided information regarding the risks of treatments by their doctors; Faden & Beauchamp, 1986). That is to say, before the period of informed consent, doctors and patients did talk to each other and consent was legally required and generally obtained.

SIMPLE CONSENT

This practice of consent during the pre-informed consent era has been called "simple consent" (Grisso & Appelbaum, 1998). In both simple and informed consent, it is expected that doctors would disclose something to patients about their medical situation and obtain their consent before proceeding with the treatment. But there are differences between the two models of consent in their underlying conceptions of the doctor–patient relationship. In simple consent, the doctor is presumed to know what is best for the patient, and the role for the patient is not to evaluate for herself the elements necessary for a medical decision but rather to accept or to refuse the expert's recommendation. The legal basis for requiring consent in the era of simple consent was the common law of battery. The reason that a surgeon had to obtain consent before operating on a patient was not because he was obligated to facilitate an autonomous decision by the patient (in the sense of the patient herself weighing the particulars of the treatment situation) but rather because to operate without consent would constitute a violation, an unwanted touching.

During the preinformed consent era, the doctor determined what was good for the patients to know, even if it meant deceiving them (Faden & Beauchamp, 1986). In fact, it is this welfare-based (rather than autonomy-based) model of the doctor–patient relationship that dictated the content of disclosures (of risks and benefits of a proposed treatment) that doctors provided to patients in the simple consent era. For instance, in the *Slater v. Baker and Stapleton* (1767) case, the court not only stated the requirement of consent but also said, "It is reasonable that a patient should be told what is about to be done to him ..."; but the court then gives the rationale as "that he may take courage and put himself in such a situation as to enable him to undergo the operation."

INFORMED CONSENT

The modern notion of informed consent assumes a different conception of the doctor–patient relationship. The patient's role is not simply to accept or refuse a treatment already determined by the physician, but to consider and process for herself the information relevant for medical decision making. The legal evolution of the informed consent doctrine is not a story of the presence or absence of patient self-determination as a value, but as a story of the expansion of the nature and limits of patient self-determination. Even simple consent was recognized to be based on the value of self-determination. Even simple consent was recognized to be based on the value of self-determination. Beginning with a series of cases in the early 20th century, with the most famous being *Schloendorff v. Society of New York Hospitals* (1914), U.S. courts articulated self-determination as the basis for requiring consent:

> Every human being of adult years and sound mind has the right to determine what shall be done with his own body; and a surgeon who performs an operation without her patient's consent commits an assault, for which she is liable in damages.

Note that this famous emphasis on self-determination is still coupled with the notion of simple consent, because what is violated here is not the patient's rightful *informed* decision-making authority but rather the patient's body ("commits an assault").

It was not until the 1950s–1970s that courts began to delineate more fully the "informed" part of informed consent. In *Salgo v. Leland Stanford Jr. University Board of Trustees* (1957), the court said physicians have a duty to disclose "any facts which are necessary to *form the basis of an intelligent consent* by the patient to proposed treatment" (italics added). In *Natanson v. Kline* (1960), the Kansas Supreme Court enumerated the various elements of the decision-making situation that a doctor must disclose to the patient. It became necessary for doctors to disclose the nature of the condition and its proposed treatment, its risks and benefits, and the alternatives to treatment and their potential outcomes, including the option of not treating at all (*Natanson v. Kline*, 1960). This list of course has a familiar ring because it has largely been preserved in the modern disclosure requirement of informed consent for treatment. This marked a major expansion of the role of the patient in medical decision making. The rationale for consent is not simply to agree to an expert's recommendation, but rather to allow the patient to take part in the medical decision-making process itself to a degree that was unprecedented before the informed consent era.

CASE LAW

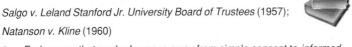

Salgo v. Leland Stanford Jr. University Board of Trustees (1957);
Natanson v. Kline (1960)

- Early cases that marked a move away from simple consent to *informed* consent.

But the scope of the patient's self-determination is still somewhat limited in *Salgo* and in *Natanson*. Both courts deferred to the medical profession to define specifically how the disclosure should be offered. This established what is now called the *professional standard* for the content of disclosures. Basically, doctors had the leeway to decide specifically what to disclose and how to disclose it. But this standard of disclosure was challenged in *Canterbury v. Spence* (1972) and other cases (e.g., *Cobbs v. Grant*, 1972), replacing it with a *patient-centered standard*. The *Canterbury* case is worth quoting at some length, because the court's decision is widely regarded as central to the evolution of the concept of informed consent:

> The duty to disclose, we have reasoned, arises from phenomena apart from medical custom and practice. The latter, we think, should no more establish the scope of the duty than its existence. Any definition of scope in terms purely of a professional standard is at odds with the patient's prerogative to decide on the projected therapy himself. That prerogative, we have said, is at the very foundation of the duty to disclose, and both the patient's right to know and the physician's correlative obligation to tell him are diluted to the extent that its compass is dictated by the medical profession. (*Canterbury v. Spence*, 1972)

Thus the court explicitly repudiated the traditional beneficence-based rationale for disclosure in stating that the duty to disclose does not arise from "medical custom and practice" (as it would be if it were done as part of the doctor's role to promote the patient's welfare), but instead arises from "the patient's prerogative to decide." In the *Canterbury* case, the court decided that the disclosure standard should be a patient-centered standard—what an "average, reasonable patient" would need to know. The language of the court clearly shows that the scope of the patient's self-determination has now gone beyond agreeing or disagreeing with a physician's recommendations; the patient now has a "right to know."

Some courts and jurisdictions have taken this logic even further, going beyond a *reasonable persons standard* (sometimes called the "objective" patient-centered standard) and adopting a "subjective" patient-centered standard in which the standard of disclosure is not determined by what would be important to a reasonable patient but to the particular patient in question (Berg et al., 2001). As of 2002,

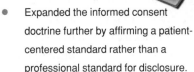

CASE LAW

Canterbury v. Spence (1972)

● Expanded the informed consent doctrine further by affirming a patient-centered standard rather than a professional standard for disclosure.

a slight majority of the states and the District of Columbia have adopted some form—almost always using the objective standard—of a patient-centered standard of disclosure, by statute or by a controlling case (Studdert et al., 2007). The trend in the literature and in policies recently adopted by jurisdictions outside the United States favors some form of a patient-centered standard (Studdert et al., 2007). In bioethics writings, one can find endorsements of the subjective patient-centered standard as ethically superior to the objective patient-centered (reasonable person) standard, as one prominent clinical ethics textbook put it: "The reasonable person standard may be ethically sufficient, but the subjective standard is ethically ideal" (Jonsen, Siegler, & Windslade, 1998, p. 55).

Sociocultural Forces, the Rise of Bioethics, and Other Legal Developments

Legal developments in informed consent did not occur in a vacuum. The legal cases that shaped informed consent probably would not have had staying power if they had not had the support of a broader cultural milieu. It is no accident that the *Canterbury v. Spence* ruling occurred around the time of notable social shifts of the 1960s and the 1970s, which in general favored the individual over the institutional and cultural powers, as exemplified in the civil rights and women's rights movements, the famous privacy cases leading to *Roe v. Wade* and the consumer movement, among others.

Among the most important of these trends was the emergence of "bioethics." As per one influential "insider" account of the history of bioethics, five major problems or issues led the way to the birth of bioethics: (a) ethics of human subject research, (b) ethics of genetics, (c) organ transplantation, (d) death and dying controversies, and (e) ethics of human reproduction (Jonsen, 1998). Perhaps the greatest impetus for the rise of the modern doctrine of informed consent was the ethics of human subject research. In the research context, the doctrine of informed consent had a much earlier start, even if at times its practice tragically lagged behind theory. Even prior to the Nuremburg Court's focus on Nazi experiments, the notion of informed consent (even if not explicitly stated as such) was a much more obvious issue when it came to consent for research. It was recognized early on that conducting research on human subjects created a different dynamic: the primary goal of research is the creation of knowledge rather than welfare of the subjects. By the late 1960s, the independent, institutionalized ethical oversight—that is, external regulation—of research protocols had begun (Jonsen, 1998). Because the ethics of research involving the decisionally impaired remains an active ethico-legal issue and is likely to grow in importance, it is discussed in more detail in chapter 8.

The development of the informed consent doctrine in turn brought about other legal changes that expanded the patient's right to self-determination in other areas of medicine. Perhaps the most notable were a series of cases on the right to refuse treatment. In mental health law, the legal standard for involuntary commitment had been the presumed need for treatment, a standard that fit well with a more paternalistic, welfare-based rationale. This standard was replaced by the "dangerousness to self or to others" criteria for involuntary commitment (Appelbaum, 1994). This change created a new question: Can involuntarily committed patients (whose commitment was not based on competency considerations) be compelled to take psychotropic medications? A series of rulings have affirmed that just because a person is involuntarily committed does not imply, by that fact, that she also forgoes the right to refuse treatment (*Rennie v. Klein*, 1978; *Rivers v. Katz*, 1986; *Rogers v. Okin*, 1979).

In addition to the mental health law developments, the right to refuse treatment, even life-sustaining treatments, became well established in law during the period following the development of the informed consent doctrine. In fact, the U.S. Supreme Court

Cruzan v. Director, Missouri Department of Health, 496 U.S. 261 (1990) firmly recognized a constitutionally protected liberty interest of competent patients to refuse treatments even though it would mean that they would die.

Legal Standards

Informed Versus Simple Consent: Implications for Capacity Evaluations

The legal developments in the doctrine of informed consent, as well as the generally increased emphasis on the principle of autonomy in medical ethics and in other areas of health law, have important implications for the evaluation of treatment consent capacity. The most important of these is that the modern doctrine of informed consent requires what might be called a *functionalist model of competence.*

A functionalist model of capacity means that a person's capacity status is determined by his demonstrable abilities— "that which an individual can do or accomplish, as well as to the knowledge, understanding or beliefs that may be necessary" (Grisso, 2003, pp. 23–24)—rather than by some type of diagnostic status or label such as "an unsound mind." This may seem obvious until one remembers that the model of simple consent did not require a robust, function-based concept of competence because that ability—that is, medical decision-making—was not expected of the patient. An intuitive understanding of having a "sound mind" was all that was needed. There was no need for an elaborate doctrine or practice of determining competence in the days when physicians' opinions were paramount and required little by way of explanation. Indeed, in the 19th century, to be mentally ill was sufficient to deprive a person of her decisional authority, without any regard for what the person might or might not actually be able to do (Appelbaum & Grisso, 1995).

In contrast, the modern doctrine of informed consent with its specific requirements for disclosure implies a need for a function-based model for assessing consent capacity. The point behind providing comprehensive disclosure is that patients are seen as capable of using the information to arrive at an autonomous decision. This probably explains why so many of the statutes (see next section) tend to focus on the type of information that the patient is expected to handle competently (i.e., the disclosure elements that cases such as *Natanson* required).

Legal Standards of Capacity

What are the relevant functional abilities, if possessed to a sufficient degree, that render a person legally capable of making his own informed consent decision? The clinician evaluator seeking concrete, detailed guidance in statutes or case law will be disappointed. Instead, the criteria for capacity tend to be broadly stated with little explanation. Moreover, there are jurisdictional variations. Sometimes the same terms are used to refer to different concepts. A brief discussion with examples will illustrate these points.

In most writings on the doctrine of informed consent—whether they be scholarly writings, statutes, case law, or commission reports—references to and discussions of standards for capacity are fairly broad. Some definitions are virtually tautological: " 'Incapable' means that in the opinion of the court in a proceeding to appoint or confirm authority of a health care representative, or in the opinion of the principal's attending physician, a principal *lacks the ability to make and communicate health care decisions* to health care providers…" (Oregon Health Care Decisions Act, 1993). Such a definition is almost entirely procedural, deferring to the judgment of the court or the attending physician. In effect, incapacity is whatever the person empowered to determine capacity says it is.

Other statutes and case law definitions go a step further by breaking down "decision-making capacity" into some elemental components. For example, the New York Health Care Proxy Law defines treatment consent capacity as "the ability to understand and appreciate the nature and consequences of health care decisions, including the benefits and risks of and alternatives to any proposed health care, and to reach an informed decision" (1990). The Illinois Health Care Surrogate Act (2007) says, "'Decisional capacity' means the ability to understand and appreciate the nature and consequences of a decision regarding medical treatment or forgoing life-sustaining treatment and the ability to reach and communicate an informed decision in the matter." Note that "understand" and "appreciate" are not further defined in either law. In the New York law, the ability "to reach" an informed decision is stated by itself, perhaps relying on an unstated implication that for someone to know that a patient has "reached" a decision, the patient must communicate that decision, whereas the Illinois law explicitly refers to "ability to reach and communicate," suggesting that reaching a decision and communicating a decision might be related but somehow distinct concepts.

Outside the law, there have been commission reports and scholarly works on bioethics that have addressed the issue of criteria for capacity. The President's Commission for the Study of Ethical Problems in Medicine and Biomedical and Behavioral Research was formed by President Carter in the late 1970s. It published a report called *Making Health Care Decisions: The Ethical and Legal Implications of Informed Consent in the Patient–Practitioner Relationship* in 1982. According to the report, the "Elements of Capacity" are "(1) possession of a set of values and goals; (2) the ability to communicate and to understand information; and (3) the ability to reason and to deliberate about one's choices" (p. 57). The first criterion is sometimes called the *authenticity criterion* and is not generally found in statutes and case law (Buchanan & Brock, 1989). Buchanan and Brock (1989, pp. 23–25), who seemed to have authored the Commission's criteria, further explained their view of "the ability to communicate and to understand" (note that this is stated as a single ability) as "the ability to appreciate the nature and meaning of potential alternatives," which implies that at least their use of the term *appreciate* is different from that in the statutes from New York and Illinois cited earlier.

Another instructive example is a landmark paper by Roth, Meisel, and Lidz (1977), which is still widely cited. In those early days of the doctrine of informed consent, the authors attempted to "make sense of various tests of competency" that they saw in law and clinical practice, which at the time had not been well developed. They described five standards: (a) evidencing a choice; (b) "reasonable outcome of choice" standard, which looks to the content of the patient's choice rather than the process; (c) "rational reasons" standard; (d) "the ability to understand" standard; and (e) the "actual understanding" standard, which the authors felt "reduces competency to an epiphenomenon. . . . The competent patient is by definition one who has provided a knowledgeable consent to treatment." It is notable that what the authors call the rational reasons standard was, despite its name, a forerunner of what would become known as the appreciation standard (described in detail in chapter 2). Further, the authors were highly critical of this rational reasons standard (which is now widely accepted). The Roth et al. paper also did not identify what would later be called the "reasoning" standard (see later discussion).

Despite these apparent discrepancies in the various definitions, one should resist the tempting thought that legal standards for capacity are arbitrary. Given the functional model of competency (elaborated more fully in chapter 2), along with the various elements that must be disclosed to patients for informed consent (i.e., the nature of the illness and proposed treatment, its potential benefits and risks and their likelihood, the available alternatives and their benefits and risks), there is a limited and logical set of actions and abilities that are relevant for a competent consent to treatment. In fact, beginning with the paper by Roth et al. (1977) and continuing through the work of Appelbaum and Grisso (Appelbaum & Grisso, 1988; Appelbaum & Roth, 1982; Berg, Appelbaum, & Grisso, 1996; Grisso & Appelbaum, 1998), scholars have carefully reviewed the various statutes and case laws, as well as the bioethics and medical literature, to forge widely, if not universally, accepted concepts associated with the legal standards for capacity that are used by most clinicians in this country and elsewhere (World Health Organization, 2005). Those concepts will be reviewed in chapter 2.

Legal Procedures and the Clinical Context of Capacity Evaluations

This book is part of a series on forensic assessments, and "forensic" refers to a connection to a court of law. Is the assessment of the capacity to consent to treatment a forensic assessment in this sense? The answer is both yes and no. It is true that sometimes there must be a formal adjudication of a patient's capacity to give consent for treatment. Also, most states have statutory standards of competence (for a variety of medical decision-making situations) that clinicians are expected to use.

Difference From Other Forensic Assessments

Yet there is an important difference between other forensic assessments and the assessment of capacity for treatment consent, and this difference has important practical implications for the evaluator. To appreciate the difference, compare the evaluation of treatment consent capacity with the evaluation of a criminal defendant's competence to stand trial. The latter evaluation arises because a person is in court (on a criminal charge), and it involves interests that go beyond those of the person being examined. There is a need to balance the interests of the state (in carrying out justice) and the interests of the defendant. This is why there would be a conflict of roles if the defendant's mental health clinician were also the forensic evaluator of competence to stand trial. This kind of forensic assessment begins and ends in the courts.

In contrast, the evaluation of a patient's capacity to provide informed consent for treatment usually arises outside the legal system, and almost always from a clinical setting. Further, there is no outside interest that has to be balanced against the patient's interests. The balancing actually involves two interests of the patient—the patient's welfare interests and the patient's autonomy interests. Patients have the right to make their own decisions. But they also need to be protected from making decisions that might harm them if they do not have the capacity to make those decisions. When patients have limited capacity, honoring one of these interests inevitably risks depriving the patient of the other. But they are both the patient's interests.

In fact, for a modern clinician this is a familiar balancing act even outside of the capacity evaluation context. Clinicians have always been concerned about the health of the patient (the patient's welfare interests), but the modern clinician is also taught to weigh the patient's autonomy interests (in the form of the patient's own preferences) when deciding on a treatment option. For this reason, the concept of "shared decision making" is now ubiquitous in the clinical setting. Thus, most clinicians will experience no conflict of roles when asked to assess a patient's clinical state ("Is this patient depressed?" "Why is this person delirious?") as well as to assess that patient's decision-making capacity to consent to treatment. Integrating the patient's well-being and the patient's right to self-determination is now the ideal of modern medical practice.

As noted earlier, most capacity assessments in the clinical setting arise and are resolved without the courts becoming involved. Litigated competence proceedings for medical treatment consent capacity are rare (Garrison & Schneider, 2003). Just as modern medicine integrates the doctrine of informed consent into its everyday practice, it also integrates the evaluation of one of its components (capacity) into the clinical arena. Of course, this does not mean that all cases of capacity determinations are conducted and acted upon outside of the courts. As we will see, adjudication of competence is more common in certain settings (e.g., psychiatric inpatient units) and there are important types of cases (e.g., disputes about capacity) that require referral to courts. These cases are discussed in chapter 7. However, it is still true that in their role as consultants, mental health professionals will generally determine capacity of patients without the involvement of the courts.

INFO

Unlike in other forensic assessments, there is no conflict of interest between acting as a clinician and as a evaluator of treatment consent capacity. Indeed, the two roles should be performed together.

Capacity and Competence

Before concluding this chapter, it is important to deal with a common confusion about the terms *capacity* and *competence*. Because this book will frequently use these two terms interchangeably, an explanation is necessary.

It is often said and widely taught that *"capacity"* is a clinical concept, whereas *"competence"* is a legal one. This use of the two terms seems to derive from our need to separate the clinician's judgment about a patient's decision-making status from a court's judgment about that patient's decision-making status. Much ink is periodically spilt describing and debating this distinction (Cranston, Marson, Dymek, & Karlawish, 2001). Yet the distinction, although important, is not captured well by these two terms, and can cause unnecessary confusion.

First, courts and statutes often use the term *capacity* or even *decision-making capacity* to refer to adjudicated determination of competence. Therefore, the law itself does not reserve *capacity* only to refer to a clinician's judgment in clinical practice. We already saw in the above discussion that the term *capacity* is the legal term used in many statutes. Indeed, in the example used above, we saw that " 'incapable' means that in the opinion of the court . . . or in the opinion of the principal's attending physician" so that the law sometimes uses the *same term* for both adjudicated and clinical determinations of incapacity.

Second, the vast majority of clinical determinations of capacity have the de facto impact of adjudicated competence, because most cases do not go to court, and in everyday medical practice it is the clinician's judgment about whether the patient will be allowed to make autonomous decisions that carries the day. This is not to deny that for some medical decisions, courts must be involved (see chapter 7); but they are special circumstances rather than the general rule.

Third, it is important to remember that in most states a clinician's judgment does have explicit legal force as specified in statutes. This is one of the main dangers of the view that capacity is clinical and competence is legal, as it has the potential to downplay the actual legal force (and responsibility) of capacity determinations by clinicians. The very point of having statutes that specify and authorize attending physicians to make judgments regarding treatment consent capacity is to confer a kind of legal (even if not final) authority to their clinical judgment.

Fourth, drawing a legal line between capacity and competence also obscures the fact that the term capacity can sometimes be used to refer to the dimensional aspect of functional capacity (i.e., as a matter of degree, as in, "does this person have sufficient or enough capacity?") whereas competence tends to refer to the categorical determination ("yes or no"). Although this additional use of capacity does potentially create further confusion, it is a natural use of the term that can be easily inferred from its context of use.

As this is a book about treatment consent capacity, the unqualified uses of terms *capacity, decision-making capacity,* and *competence* are all meant to refer to that capacity. Thus, *capacity* and *competence* will be used interchangeably. When a court's determination of capacity is specifically meant, it will be referred to as "adjudicated capacity [or competence]," if the context does not make that apparent already. Indeed, in general the context of the usage will make the meanings obvious, and if this is not the case, specific qualifiers will be used.

Forensic Mental Health Concepts

2

The capacity to provide informed consent to treatment is a legal concept based on case law and specific statutes arising out of the doctrine of informed consent (Berg et al., 1996; Garrison & Schneider, 2003). In applying this legal concept, it is useful to remember that law cannot specify ahead of time fully operational criteria for what is admittedly an abstract and broad concept. It leaves room for judgment. This is a common feature of definitions of legal competencies (Grisso, 2003). Over the years, clinicians have filled in this interpretive space and what has emerged over time is a practice (or a variety of practices) that is informed and delimited by law but interpreted through the lens of ethical considerations and the principles of good clinical practice.

This chapter examines how the law has been interpreted and incorporated into the practice of capacity evaluations in two parts. First, it turns to the topic of standards or definitions of capacity that legally define the concept, and provides a framework for interpreting and implementing them in a way that is consistent with law and is clinically useful. Second, the chapter discusses what might be called the pillars of the modern concept of capacity for treatment consent. These are the principles of practice that have emerged in the assessment of treatment consent capacity but that are not explicitly enumerated in legal definitions of competence. They comprise the currently accepted interpretive framework for the practice of evaluating treatment consent capacity.

Abilities Relevant to Treatment Consent Capacity

The model with the most widespread acceptance in practice—which will be referred to as the "four standards" or "four abilities" model—has been developed over the past two decades by Paul

Appelbaum, Thomas Grisso, and colleagues (Appelbaum & Grisso, 1995, 1988; Appelbaum & Roth, 1982; Berg et al., 1996; Grisso & Appelbaum, 1998). There are good reasons for using the four abilities model. First, the model is based on a comprehensive review of statutory and case law, as well as important scholarly sources and commission reports (Berg et al., 1996). Second, there are more empirical research data based on this model than on any other; the model therefore allows a more evidence-based approach to competency assessment than do other models. Third, the model is comprehensive enough to accommodate a variety of definitions of capacity, and flexible enough to accommodate important moral intuitions regarding competence. For any given standard that is mentioned in the law or in court cases or in organizational policies, one can make a reasonable application of one or a combination of the standards to cover the particular definition. This is a crucial point. It means that with a sound understanding of the four abilities model, one can, so to speak, take advantage of the ethical and legal groundwork underlying the model as well as the increasing amount of empirical data based on the model.

The four abilities or standards are (a) the ability to evidence a choice, (b) the ability to understand, (c) the ability to appreciate, and (d) the ability to reason. The following discussion consists of the essential definitional elements of each standard. Chapter 5 provides guidance on how to assess these abilities in a capacity interview, and chapter 6 discusses some of the more difficult interpretive situations that arise regarding these standards.

The Ability to Evidence a Choice

The ability to evidence or communicate a choice requires the patient to merely indicate a decision regarding a treatment or procedure. The reasons or the processes by which the patient arrives at the choice are not included in the concept. The mere communication of the choice is sufficient. As such, it is best understood as a necessary but insufficient basis for competence in most instances. Without it the patient is incompetent; with it, the person may or may not be competent. The concept of communicating a choice probably corresponds to the notions of assent and dissent that is

BEWARE
The ability to
communicate a choice
is necessary but not sufficient
to establish capacity. 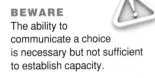 often talked about in other contexts (National Bioethics Advisory
Commission, 1998).

Despite the apparent simplicity
of this standard, there are some key
issues to remember. First, the ability to communicate a choice does
not require that the person be able to express the choice verbally.
Obviously, just because a person is on a ventilator does not mean that
she is unable to communicate a choice. Second, despite its simplicity,
patients can fail to meet the standard in a variety of ways. The most
obvious is an unconscious person from whom there is no communication at all. But other examples are persons in a catatonic state who
are nearly or entirely mute, or whose negativity (i.e., automatic and
indiscriminate negative answers to a variety of questions and resistance to physical maneuvers) is such that the refusal of a treatment or
procedure is better characterized as a nonvoluntary utterance arising
out of brain dysfunction, rather than as an expression of choice.
Further, sometimes this standard comes into play even when the
patient apparently communicates a choice:

> A middle-aged man with schizophrenia was admitted to the cardiac
> unit in a general hospital after an episode of syncope, and was found
> to need a cardiac pacemaker. The attending cardiologist explained
> the situation to the patient who agreed to the pacemaker placement.
> Early next morning, the cardiology fellow came in to obtain a signed
> informed consent before taking the patient "to the operating room."
> The patient refused. Later in the day, the attending cardiologist
> again came by and the patient again agreed, only to refuse again
> the following morning. This occurred three times. The psychiatric
> consultation service was called to assess the patient's treatment
> consent capacity. It was determined that the patient lacked the
> capacity to consent to the procedure. One reason was that the
> patient lacked the ability to communicate a choice because his
> choice was not stable enough to actually carry out the procedure.

The ability to communicate a choice therefore assumes a certain
amount of stability in the choice. If the choice flip-flops such that
the decision cannot be carried out, it is unclear that the patient is

making a meaningful choice at all. Of course, like many aspects of capacity evaluation, the evaluator must exercise some judgment about just how stable the choice must be, but the functional standard of "stable enough to carry out the decision" is a useful rule.

Thus the criterion of evidencing or communicating a choice, although initially seeming to be a rather basic requirement, has some substance to it. For the person to be able to meet the standard, she must be capable of recognizing that a question is being posed to her (and so the standard assumes a certain amount of intact language ability) and that she is being asked to render a choice; she must be able to communicate a choice that is in fact one of the options available and must be stable enough for the choice to be implemented.

The Ability to Understand

The ability to understand the information that is disclosed in informed consent discussions is perhaps the most intuitive standard, and indeed some version of it is present in all discussions of competency standards and in all legal definitions of capacity (Berg et al., 1996). The ability to understand is broader than a mere retention and regurgitation of what the doctor tells the patient. The patient must be able to "grasp the fundamental meaning" (Appelbaum, 2007) of the disclosed information. The four abilities model uses a slightly technical and narrower definition of understanding that does not require a belief in the disclosed information on the part of the patient. (This is explained further in "The Ability to Appreciate" section.) Instead, it focuses on what might best be described as intellectual, factual comprehension.

The Ability to Appreciate

The ability to appreciate refers to patients' ability to apply the facts that are disclosed to them. Thus appreciation can be truly assessed only if understanding is intact. Indeed, often in the clinical setting, doctors use the term "understand" in a broader, more colloquial sense to include both factual understanding of information and an application of those facts to one's own situation. In order to be able to appreciate the medical facts as they apply to them, patients must be able to form accurate beliefs. The distinction between factual comprehension and forming beliefs regarding those facts is best illustrated with an example:

> A 50-year-old woman had a delusional belief that she was suffering from a systemic fungal infection. After all the tests revealed that she was not infected, the attending physician from the infectious disease service explained the results to the patient. Later, when asked whether she understood what she was told, she was able to clearly recount and even explain all the facts that the physician had disclosed to her. However, she refused to believe what she had been told and persisted in her belief that she was infected.

2
chapter

The ability to understand is an intellectual capacity to comprehend the facts at hand. It does not require the patient to state a belief or disbelief in the facts. Again, this is a somewhat narrower way of using the term than is sometimes used in the clinic, as clinicians often include both understanding and appreciation when they ask patients whether they understand the clinical situation.

The ability to appreciate encompasses two broad domains: "whether patients (1) acknowledge, or appreciate, that they are suffering from the disorder with which they have been diagnosed, and (2) acknowledge the consequences of the disorder and of potential treatment options for their own situation" (Grisso & Appelbaum, 1998, pp. 42–43). But the lack of appreciation does not simply refer to the lack of belief in one's medical condition or its potential consequences with and without treatment. *The basis or cause of that lack of belief* must meet certain criteria for the patient to be deemed to lack appreciation (Grisso & Appelbaum, 1998, pp. 45–49).

Specifically, the evaluator needs to assess whether the apparent lack of appreciation is due to (a) a belief that can reasonably be deemed defective, or, "substantially irrational, unrealistic, or a considerable distortion of reality" (p. 45); (b) the belief must be due to an impairment in functioning, cognitive or affective; *and* (c) the belief actually seems to affect the lack of appreciation, rather than being some extraneous belief unconnected to the treatment decision at hand.

BEWARE
Whether a patient lacks appreciation is not simply a matter of whether the patient lacks a requisite belief—much depends on the nature and cause of the lack.

The Ability to Reason

Even if patients understand and appreciate the facts of their clinical situation, some process must connect the factual understanding, the beliefs surrounding that understanding, and the outcome of expressing a preference. Court decisions may refer to "rational thought processes" or "give rational reasons" or statutes refer to the ability "to reach a decision" in order to capture this process that is involved in manipulating the information that is presented to the patients. This is the ability to reason component of treatment consent capacity.

There are several key points to remember with regard to the ability to reason. First, the standard does not refer to the reasonableness of the decision made by the patient. Although a very unconventional decision (say, refusing a treatment with high benefit but no burden) may trigger closer scrutiny (perhaps leading to an evaluation), the "reasonableness" of the content of a choice cannot be the sole basis for judging someone incompetent. Such an outcome-based standard was described (and criticized) among the five standards reviewed in the landmark article by Roth et al. (1977), and some researchers still use it for research purposes with an explicit caveat against its use in practice (Marson, Ingram, Cody, & Harrell, 1995b). But it should not be considered a legitimate standard because it obviously is in direct contradiction with the modern concept of a patient's self-determination reviewed in chapter 1.

Second, the reasoning standard is not actually a single standard or ability but a variety of abilities that have to do with the formal decision-making process. Another way to think about this is that there are many processes that can all be called a form of reasoning. An obvious one is logical consistency: if a patient endorses two contradictory statements regarding a medical decision, this is evidence against competence (although recent evidence suggests that patients with schizophrenia may actually do quite well on deductive reasoning tasks) (Owen, Cutting, & David, 2007). Appelbaum and Grisso, in constructing their capacity instruments, designed methods for assessing various facets of reasoning as found in the psychological literature on "decision

BEWARE
The "reasonableness" of the content of the patient's decision is not an accepted standard for determining the patient's ability to reason.

making or problem solving" (Grisso, Appelbaum, Mulvey, & Fletcher, 1995). Thus, the reasoning section of these instruments was constructed not so much based on statutory or case law definitions (as was the case for understanding and appreciation) but rather on inferred constructs from psychology of decision making and problem solving (Grisso & Appelbaum, 1998; Grisso et al., 1995). They incorporate concepts of "comparative reasoning" and "consequential reasoning" in the various instruments that measure reasoning (Appelbaum & Grisso, 2001; Grisso, Appelbaum, & Hill-Fotouhi, 1997). Elsewhere, these authors have enumerated the following abilities as relevant to the reasoning standard: ability to stay focused on the decision task, ability to consider the options, ability to consider and imagine consequences, ability to assess the likelihood of consequences, ability to weigh desirability of consequences in light of one's values, ability to deliberate by taking all of these factors into account to reach a decision (Grisso & Appelbaum, 1998, pp. 54–55). The main point here is that there are many different types of suboptimal "processing" in making a decision, and that when it is severe enough, it can make someone incompetent.

Third, the reasoning standard should be applied to how the patient reasons in making the decision at hand. A patient who reasons normally regarding the medical decision at issue but shows many contradictions regarding some other area of decision making need not on the latter's account be deemed incompetent. It is an empirical matter whether such a discrepancy could exist, but it is possible. One could argue that many people have particular blind spots in their lives in which rational thinking is notably absent, or even irrational thinking dominant. But an assessment of their reasoning ability must be restricted to its role in the medical decision at hand.

Finally, the reasoning standard should not be used alone. It is not as commonly delineated by the courts or statutes and, according to Berg et al. (1996) is never used alone by the courts but rather always in conjunction with other standards. This has important practical implications as it means that the capacity evaluator will not (and should not) generally rely on the failure of the reasoning standard as the sole criterion for determining someone as incompetent (see chapter 5 discussion on how this affects the capacity interview). Indeed, as will be seen in discussions below, in practice the evaluation of the reasoning standard often serves as probes for uncovering deficiencies in appreciation and understanding.

Are the Four Abilities Enough?

This question can be relevant in two senses. One, given the myriad of definitions of competence, are the concepts within the four abilities model sufficient to account for all of the standards enumerated by the courts, statutes, and organizational policies? Two, what should be done about other standards that are often mentioned in the literature but are (apparently) not included in the four abilities model?

Making Sense of the Variety of Standards

Despite its broad acceptance within the psychiatric community in the United States, most statutes, various ethico-legal writings, and policies that might affect the work of the clinician do not *explicitly* enumerate the four abilities model. Indeed, the reader will find that his facility's institutional policy on decision-making capacity will state the elements of competence in such a way that the extent of overlap with the four abilities model may not be self-evident.

Fortunately, most standards enumerated in policies and statutes are consistent with one or more of the standards of the four abilities model because the model is based on a comprehensive review of laws and relevant literature (Berg et al., 1996). And when the model cannot be reconciled with the standards within a jurisdiction, that in itself is important information for the capacity evaluator. The following discussion can be a guide for a capacity evaluator whose jurisdiction's definitions do not seem to match the four abilities model.

One common formulation, such as is found in NY Health Care Proxy law, defines "decision-making capacity" as "the ability to understand and appreciate the nature and consequences of health care decisions, including the benefits and risks of and alternatives to any proposed health care, and to reach an informed decision" (1990). There are three abilities cited in this law: "to understand" and to "appreciate" and "to reach an informed decision." The remainder is in fact a paraphrase of the familiar disclosure elements for informed consent. It seems reasonable to use the four abilities model's definition of understanding and appreciation in this case; the same terms are used, and the inclusion of both terms (assuming they are not intended to be redundant) suggests that it comports with the distinctions in the four abilities model. The ability "to reach" an informed decision appears to describe a process that occurs between understanding and appreciating the information to the decision at issue; it seems reasonable to interpret this intervening process as what "reasoning" refers to in the four abilities model. It is true that this NY law does not explicitly mention "evidencing a choice," and other states that have otherwise identical definitions as New York use "to reach and communicate an informed decision" instead (e.g., Illinois Health Care Surrogate Act, 2007). But it seems a bit of a stretch to read the NY law to mean that a person need not be able to communicate her choice to be competent.

A slightly more challenging situation is the new law passed in England and Wales called the Mental Capacity Act (2005), which took effect in 2007. This law is worth examining because it comes from a nation that shares a similar common law history, and it is one of the most recent pieces of legislation on the topic in an English-speaking jurisdiction. The Act defines a person as unable to make his own decision if he fails (a) to understand the information relevant to the decision; (b) to retain that information; (c) to use or weigh that information as part of the process of making the decision; or (d) to communicate his decision (whether by talking, using sign language, or any other means). Conditions (c) and (d) seem a reasonable statement of the reasoning standard and the evidencing a choice standard. Condition (b) is in some degree implied by the concept of "understanding necessary for decision making" as some amount of temporal continuity is necessary for making a decision and the law explicitly says that "the fact that a person is able to retain the information relevant to a decision for a short period only does not prevent him from being regarded as able to make the decision." So the question becomes whether condition (a) should be construed to encompass both understanding and appreciation or only understanding in the narrow sense. How should one interpret condition (a)? There are accompanying guidance documents explaining the new law (Department for Constitutional Affairs, 2007), a luxury that does not commonly exist when interpreting statutes. The accompanying documents do not explicitly split the two components of "understanding" and "belief/acknowledgment" (in effect, appreciation). But the discussions involving the lack of insight in a head-injured man suggest that the term understanding as used in the law includes belief; that is, the law seems to be using a broad definition of understanding that includes appreciation. Further, the new law is meant to be consistent with "existing common law tests" of capacity, making it likely that it is not written to explicitly forbid the use of the appreciation standard. A capacity evaluator who must make her determination using the Mental Capacity Act would therefore be acting in conformity with the new law if she states that a patient lacks understanding of relevant information if the patient fails to appreciate his own condition or the consequences of the various treatment options as they apply to his situation.

In general, most of the standards or abilities discussed fall under a short list and tend to overlap and can be reasonably interpreted to overlap. For example, no one would dispute that an essential ability is the ability to comprehend the key disclosure elements of informed consent. It is often the case that this simple concept may be expressed in different ways, but the core concept remains the same. This is where the Grisso–Appelbaum four abilities model is very useful, as it captures the essential common elements.

But there are some standards for competence that hold intuitive appeal and have been proposed by more than one source, but their application needs further clarification. One such standard is the so-called authenticity criterion.

Authenticity and Competence

Because the notion of authenticity as a criterion for consent capacity repeatedly arises in some influential documents and writings, it is important to see just where authenticity fits into the overall scheme of capacity evaluations (Buchanan & Brock, 1989; Elliott, 1997; Faden & Beauchamp, 1986, pp. 262ff; President's Commission for the Study of Ethical Problems in Medicine and Biomedical and Behavioral Research, 1982, pp. 57–58). Must a patient's choice be authentic for that decision to be deemed a competent choice? Of course, it depends on the meaning of "authentic." The influential President's Commission (1982, p. 57) report simply states that decision-making capacity requires "possession of a set of values and goals." The implication is that a patient's competent choice must reflect or be consistent with her enduring values and goals. On the surface, this standard has an intuitive appeal that seems to value the patient's autonomy. For example, it seems an important antidote to the paternalistic doctor whose own values may favor a more aggressive treatment and who may as a result tend to see the patient who refuses that treatment as incompetent. In such a case, it is appealing to think that if the patient's choice is based on his "core values," then one can be more confident of his competence.

Faden and Beauchamp (1986), in their landmark work on informed consent, noted that there are influential philosophical theories of autonomy with strong emphasis on authenticity as a necessary ingredient. As autonomy is the philosophical basis for informed consent, it makes sense to consider whether the evaluation of capacity needs to include an authenticity criterion as an independent criterion in addition to the four standards. In such a view, authenticity requires that "actions faithfully represent the values, attitudes, motivations, and life plans that the individual personally accepts upon due consideration of the way he or she wishes to live" (Faden & Beauchamp, 1986, p. 263). The concept of authenticity does indeed capture an important moral intuition about what constitutes competent decision making. However, as explained subsequently, this intuition is best captured within the four abilities model, and does not require a strong, stand-alone standard of authenticity. A strong version of authenticity criterion has implications that are inconsistent with accepted practices.

A strong definition of authenticity requires a positive and extensive evidence of authenticity as a prerequisite for competence. But there are problems with this definition.It idealizes the way people endorse and adopt values as one that occurs self-consciously and transparently and ignores some simple facts about real people. The degree of self-knowledge and the ability to articulate one's values vary greatly. Being psychologically minded or being verbally nimble may be valued by some, but not by all. Sometimes people wear their relevant core values on their sleeves, as when a Jehovah's Witness makes known her religion, but more often than not, it is not clear. And some people may reflectively endorse certain values after due consideration but others may simply endorse them without much thought. But this does not mean that those making these less deliberative, less articulate, or less coherent decisions are not competent.

Another problem with such a strong version of the authenticity criterion is that it idealizes the consistency and integration of values. It tends to idealize the internal consistency of people's values when in fact it is quite normal for people to often have conflicting values; people can be ambivalent even about important things, and this is taken as normal. Further, the idea that a person must have a "life plan" in order to be authentic and autonomous seems too high a standard for capacity. It would seem people make competent decisions every day without a coherent life plan in place.

Finally, this strong authenticity criterion tends to idealize our ability to discover and to evaluate others' core values and the relationship between those values and actual choices. Because many core values may not be transparent even to the patient, it seems a tall task for the capacity evaluator to find out. Further, it seems unduly intrusive to allow a capacity evaluator to hold another person to such a high standard of personal integration and to be given permission to probe and evaluate the strength and coherence of that integration.

Authenticity Criterion Implicit in the Four Abilities Model

Should the authenticity criterion be ignored altogether? Actually, the four abilities model probably captures the moral intuition behind the authenticity criterion, without the pitfalls of the strong version of the authenticity requirement. The President's Commission report (1982, p. 58), in explicating the meaning of the authenticity criterion, tends to emphasize the stability of the values out of which a patient's preferences arise: "Reliance on a patient's decision would be difficult or impossible if the patient's values were so unstable that the patient could not reach or adhere to a choice at least long enough for a course of therapy to be initiated with some prospect of being completed." Practically speaking, such a concern would be well addressed by the standard of evidencing a stable choice.

Recall also that in the definition of the ability to appreciate—although it was not labeled as such—there is indeed a version of an authenticity criterion embedded in it when a patient's illness-inspired delusion or irrational belief is properly seen as not really reflecting his real self. Indeed, in some cases persons with severe depression may fail to meet the appreciation standard because of their excessive and nihilistic pessimism. In a sense, their depression-based nihilism could lead to an inauthentic decision (see the "Affective Competence and Authenticity" section below). Also, in their discussion on the ability to reason, Grisso and Appelbaum (1998, p. 55) specify the ability "to weigh the desirability of various potential consequences, based on one's own subjective values" as an ability that may be subsumed under the reasoning standard.

Thus, an assessment of authenticity is inevitably a part of the assessment of treatment consent capacity using the four abilities model. Broadly speaking, the more the patient's decision is at odds with who the patient is or is known to be, the stronger the case that the decision is not authentic. But just exactly where the line ought to be drawn probably cannot be neatly summarized in an a priori definition of authenticity. Thus, rather than attempting to define a separate criterion—especially a criterion that is not explicitly addressed by the courts and statutes—it may be more useful, and no less appropriate, to address the authenticity criterion within the prevailing four abilities model of capacity. This has the advantage of capturing the value of authenticity with standards that have long been used successfully in the clinic.

Affective Competence and Authenticity

Some authors have argued that conceptualizations of consent capacity that is too cognitive may neglect the affective, valuing side of persons (Elliott, 1997). Such authors have expressed concern that some methods of assessing capacity may fail because they may miss the fact that "if a person is depressed, he or she may be *aware* that a protocol carries risks, but simply not *care* about those risks." The worry here is that unless the ability to value is seen as part of one's definition of capacity, there is the danger of missing an important basis for determining someone incompetent.

This is an important consideration. A patient may understand—that is, intellectually comprehend—the magnitude and probability of harm (or benefit) but this may not determine her evaluative attitude toward that risk or benefit. There is probably a wide range of attitudes that are normal. Some patients may highly value a 20% probability of benefit, whereas others in the same situation may not feel optimistic even with 50% probability of benefit. Some patients may tolerate a 30% chance of death in an operation whereas some patients may forgo surgery even if the chance of death is 2%. Given these considerations, is it the case that the four abilities model is conceptually unable to address the concern? It appears that one could make a strong argument that the four abilities model, especially the appreciation standard, could accommodate most of the concern. A severely depressed patient may very well be able to cognitively discuss the probabilities and nature of risks and benefits of a proposed treatment, and yet be nihilistic about it. He simply may not care about living or dying, or may see himself as unworthy and blameworthy. But the assessment of such negative attitudes, if determined to be a manifestation of the patient's depression, should be a part of the evaluation of the patient's ability to appreciate the facts of his situation. An example of how to interpret the appreciation standard in such a situation is discussed in chapter 6, and a systematic method of assessing appreciation is outlined in chapter 5.

Pillars of Modern Practice of Treatment Consent Capacity Assessment

As the doctrine of informed consent essentially arose out of an evolving view of the boundaries of medical decision making (i.e., expanding the scope of a patient's decision-making domain, and restricting the professional's role), it should not be surprising that the concept of competence embedded in the doctrine is a functional one that focuses on that expanded domain of decision making by the patient. Specifically, informed consent for a treatment assumes that a patient will competently use the information disclosed by the health care provider. The concept of capacity therefore focuses on the patient's capacity to use the disclosed information to arrive at a free choice, rather than on some feature of the person like diagnosis, age, legal status, or a quasi-psychological concept that functions as a proxy for "normal" (e.g., "being of sound mind").

This functional concept of capacity has several dimensions. The most obvious dimension is that there are several abilities (such as the ones just reviewed) that a patient must possess in order to provide valid informed consent. But a capacity evaluation is more than an assessment of the individual abilities. How those standards are applied in a capacity determination relies on other important principles of practice that have evolved over the years. The remainder of this chapter describes these key practice principles. These principles are not written into law, but rather have arisen in the practice of applying the law.

Capacity Incorporates the Patient's Function in Context

Although the modern concept of capacity is a functional one, this does not mean that it can be assessed simply by looking at the patient's abilities alone. In fact, the determination of capacity takes into account both the patient's abilities and the context in which she is expected to exercise those abilities. This is why, in their pioneering work, Buchanan and Brock (1989) stated that a person's capacity to provide informed consent is a *relational* concept. It is not simply about the decisional abilities of the person, but rather about the relationship between two concepts—a person's functional abilities and the context (such as the risks–benefit profile of the choices in question) in which he is expected to exercise those abilities. For this reason, it is best to think of this modern framework of competence as a "function-context" model of competence.

Competence Is Function and Decision Specific

One can occasionally still see articles in mainstream medical journals that treat cognitive tests as a measure of capacity status (Ferrand et al., 2001), so it may be worth repeating that what *justifies* the determination of incapacity are not the diagnoses, the poor performance on cognitive tests, or even the psychotic symptoms per se. Rather, these factors are important only in so far as they compromise the person's abilities relevant to competence. A clear understanding of the mental status of the patient is extremely important in this modern concept of competence: it is important because of its actual influence on the person's functional abilities. The fact that a person has cognitive or other mental impairment per se does not automatically mean that someone is legally incompetent, but cognitive impairment that sufficiently diminishes understanding, appreciation, reasoning, or choice may render a person incompetent.

The modern notion of capacity, because it arises out of a specific medical decision-making context and focuses on the task at issue, is a fairly restricted notion: the capacity evaluator generally does not assume that the determination of a patient's capacity applies to other contexts. It does not apply to nonmedical decisions. A person may be incapable of giving valid informed consent to a course of chemotherapy, but she may still be capable of writing a will, of driving a car, or even of providing informed consent for other medical decisions.

Contextual Aspects of Competence: Risks and Benefits of Potential Choices

Consequences matter in capacity determinations. Specifically, it is widely accepted that the level of abilities required—the threshold for competence—increases as the risk-to-benefit ratio increases. There are two important issues regarding this practice that need to be addressed: first, like other aspects of capacity evaluations, considerable judgment is required, and there is relatively little guidance on how this weighing of risks and benefits is supposed to take place; second, it must be admitted that

BEWARE
Cognitive or psychiatric symptoms or diagnoses are relevant to capacity because they may impair the patient's functional abilities to make a decision; but they do not *define* legal incompetence.

this practice raises some tensions with popular understandings of patient autonomy, and the evaluator needs to recognize and keep the grounds for the practice clear in his mind.

The President's Commission (1982) clearly endorses a sliding scale standard as does the National Bioethics Advisory Commission (1998). Yet, there are at least two reasons why some are uneasy about the practice. First, it is easy to see the potential tension between this practice and the spirit behind the informed consent doctrine, as it seems that someone other than the patient is imposing a standard of "what's good for the patient" into the evaluation; it may begin to look as if paternalism is being brought in through the backdoor.

Second, when risk–benefit consequences are incorporated into the assessment of capacity, some apparent paradoxes can occur. Consider the above example of the middle-aged man with schizophrenia who repeatedly accepted then refused a cardiac pacemaker. The treatment is life saving, and the intervention is relatively low risk, and the long-term burden is minimal. There is no need to set a very high threshold for capacity when the patient agrees. He may therefore be deemed competent. But if he refuses, then the threshold should be set higher, and in fact, it may turn out that he cannot meet that standard for capacity. The patient's abilities do not change, yet in one context he "has" capacity and in another he "lacks" it. This seems a logical contradiction. The sliding scale capacity threshold doctrine seems to accept a paradox in order to accommodate paternalistic interests. It seems incompatible with the doctrine of informed consent.

With respect to the paradox issue, it is a paradox only if one accepts a definition of "capacity" or "competence" that is nonrelational and sees it as an intrinsic feature of a person, like a person's eye color. If, however, competence is taken as a relational (i.e., relative to the context) concept and it is further recognized that a patient accepting a treatment creates a very different context for assessing that person's capacity than for refusing that treatment, then in fact there is no paradox.

Still, this response does not address the underlying concern of paternalism. Why should risk and benefits be incorporated into the context at all? Doesn't the doctrine of informed consent demand that the patient's own sense of what is desirable for herself should count, and not some external standard? Isn't the discussion above regarding the inappropriateness of a "reasonable" choice standard based precisely on this concern?

It is incontrovertible that in our society no matter how bizarre or irrational or idiosyncratic, a *competent* patient has the right to refuse any medical treatment (Meisel, 1998). But this doctrine assumes that the patient is indeed competent. The more difficult question is what to do when the patient's decision-making competence itself is in question—when it is uncertain whether the choice she is making is in fact a competent choice. The question is whether it is appropriate to use *some* concept of welfare (i.e., an assessment of the risks and potential benefits) in the determination of whether the person has capacity. To answer this question, one might ask what it would be like to ignore welfare considerations altogether, to treat minimal risk and high risk situations alike in capacity evaluations. Thus, a person who is accepting a procedure with trivial risk must exhibit the same level of capacity as a person accepting a high risk, questionable benefit procedure, or as a person refusing a life-saving treatment with little burden. These examples bring out the point that the goal of conducting a capacity evaluation is not simply to ensure that a capable patient's right to self-determination is preserved, but also to protect the incompetent from harm. Thus, a capacity determination must incorporate welfare considerations. What this shows is not that the welfare-sensitive sliding scale disregards the autonomy principle but rather that, from a societal point of view, when it comes to decisionally impaired persons (whose capacity status is uncertain), there is a strong societal interest in making sure that their welfare is protected to the extent consistent with their self-determination. And this does not violate the doctrine of informed consent.

Empirical Foundation and Limits | **3**

The last three decades have seen the emergence of the field of decision-making capacity research. The growth has been such that there are several reviews covering a variety of subtopics within the field (Dunn, Nowrangi, Palmer, Jeste, & Saks, 2006; Kim, Karlawish, & Caine, 2002b; Moye, 2003; Moye & Marson, 2007; Palmer & Savla, 2007; Sturman, 2005). Although the field remains relatively small, this is a welcome trend. The goal of this chapter is to briefly summarize the state of the research. The discussion is organized by questions that are particularly relevant for the capacity evaluator: How common is incapacity in various settings? What is the impact of neuropsychiatric and other disorders on capacity? What is the association between cognitive test results and incapacity—for example, how useful is the widely used Mini Mental State examination (MMSE) in predicting incapacity? How do clinicians behave when making capacity determinations? Can a patient's consent capacity be improved through interventions? What assessment instruments are available and how might they be used? The chapter closes with some guidance on how to interpret studies of capacity.

How Common Is Incapacity?

General Hospital

The lack of treatment consent capacity is common in general hospitals. A recent U.K. prevalence study of consecutive patients admitted to an acute medical unit over an 18-month period found that almost 48% lacked the capacity to consent to treatment

(Raymont et al., 2004). The researchers assumed that those who were unable to cooperate with an interview were incompetent. Among those who were able to be interviewed, 31% were incompetent. A Canadian general hospital study included 100 consecutive patients, excluding those unable to cooperate with interviews and also those who accepted recommended treatment and were strongly felt to be competent by the treating team. About 37% were found to be incapable (Etchells et al., 1999). Although these two studies have different methodologies, it is clear that there is a high prevalence of incapacity among the medically ill in general hospitals.

In most general hospitals, the consultation liaison (CL) psychiatry service usually performs the formal capacity evaluations requested by a treatment team. Such requests make up a significant number of consultations conducted by CL services, ranging from 3 to 25% of all psychiatric consultations (Farnsworth, 1990; Jourdan & Glickman, 1991; Knowles, Liberto, Baker, Ruskin, & Raskin, 1994; Myers & Barrett, 1986). These capacity consultations most commonly involve decisions about medical treatment, the capacity for self-care and deciding one's own disposition (Masand, Bouckoms, Fischel, Calabrese, & Stern, 1998; Ranjith & Hotopf, 2004; Umapathy, Ramchandani, Lamdan, Kishel, & Schindler, 1999).

Despite the high prevalence of incapacity in a general hospital, only a small number trigger a formal consultation. In a 10-year retrospective study in a Veterans Administration hospital, 0.2–0.4% of all admissions required a capacity consultation by the CL service (Knowles et al., 1994). The cases that are flagged for consultation end up being fairly evenly split between competent and incompetent (Farnsworth, 1990; Katz, Abbey, Rydall, & Lowy, 1995; Mebane & Rauch, 1990; Ranjith et al., 2004). This should not be surprising because, if the cases were obvious, a consultation would hardly be necessary. There are probably other reasons why patients are found to be competent in a significant proportion of consultations. A common reason for consultation is that patients refuse a recommended treatment (Masand et al., 1998) or more generally when patients pose "management problems" (Myers et al., 1986). Often such situations are driven less by competency issues as by the need for help with management of a difficult patient. Those deemed to be competent tend to have personality disorders, adjustment disorders, or no psychiatric diagnosis when they are evaluated by a consult team (Katz et al., 1995). When patients are found to be incompetent, the most common diagnoses are "organic" ones such as dementia and delirium (Farnsworth, 1990; Katz et al., 1995; McKegney, Schwartz, & O'Dowd, 1992). The rate of incapacity is higher in intensive care units (Cohen, McCue, & Green, 1993).

Nursing Homes

In a variety of studies on consent capacity conducted in nursing homes, high proportions of decisional impairment were found, ranging from 44% (Pruchno, Smyer, Rose, Hartman-Stein, & Henderson-Laribee, 1995) to 45% (Barton, Mallik, Orr, & Janofsky, 1996), 67% (Fitten, Lusky, & Hamann, 1990), and as high as 69% (Royall, Cordes, & Polk, 1997). These figures are consistent with a large, retrospective study of decision-making capacity of nursing home residents (Goodwin, Smyer, & Lair, 1995). Although the research methods differ widely among such studies, the main message is probably quite reliable and valid: incapacity is common in nursing homes.

Psychiatric Hospitals and Units

The most recent systematic review of mental capacity among psychiatric patients (Okai et al., 2007) examined whether a psychiatric inpatient has the capacity to consent to an admission or to a variety of psychiatric treatments. Studies from the United States and the United Kingdom on the capacity of psychiatric patients to consent to a psychiatric admission showed that approximately 30–50% of patients, even among voluntarily admitted patients, lacked consent capacity (Okai et al., 2007). However, one study from the United States (Appelbaum, Appelbaum, & Grisso, 1998) that

3
chapter

INFO

Lack of treatment consent capacity is common among patients in general hospitals, nursing homes, and psychiatric hospitals/units.

used a low threshold for competence that was recommended by an American Psychiatric Association Task Force found that a vast majority of the voluntarily admitted patients were competent to consent to admission. In terms of the capacity to consent to psychiatric treatment, the Okai et al. (2007) review found that of the 12 studies that met their criteria for review, the median rate of incapacity was 29% (with inter-quartile range of 22–44%).

In a recent large study from the United Kingdom published after the Okai et al. (2007) review, the researchers evaluated 338 of 350 consecutive admissions to a psychiatric unit. The patients' capacity for either consenting to admission or consenting to prescribed medications was measured by the clinical opinion of psychiatric trainees (using the four abilities model framework); of these, 200 also had their capacity assessed by a researcher using a capacity interview (MacArthur Competency Assessment Test—Treatment, MacCAT-T; Owen et al., 2008). Sixty percent were deemed incapable of consenting to either a medication decision or a psychiatric admission decision (depending on the clinical issue for the patient). Among those admitted voluntarily, 39% were deemed incapable; the rate of incapacity was 86% for the involuntarily admitted patients.

Impact of Neuropsychiatric and Other Medical Conditions

Delirium and Dementia

DELIRIUM

Delirium is an acute decline in cognition, usually accompanied by disturbance in consciousness, with impaired attention, that has a myriad of causes (Inouye, 2006). Other commonly associated features of delirium are a fluctuating course, disorganized thinking, psychotic symptoms (such as hallucinations or delusions), altered sleep–wake cycle, psychomotor hyper- or hypoactivity, and emotional lability often accompanied by dysphoria and anxiety (Inouye, 2006). Delirium is very common and signals serious morbidity; it accounts for 49% of all hospital days in the United States, and the 1-year mortality rate associated with delirium is 35–40% (Inouye, 2006). Persons with dementia—or impaired functioning in general—are at greater risk of developing delirium, and for old persons who are seriously ill, it is often a common final pathway of symptoms at the end of life.

Although delirium is very common, there have been relatively few studies that have specifically studied the relationship between delirium and capacity (Adamis, Martin, Treloar, & Macdonald, 2005; Auerswald, Charpentier, & Inouye, 1997). This may be because delirium is an acute (and fluctuating) phenomenon, and therefore more difficult to study systematically than, for example, dementia, which is a chronic condition. In a sense, because delirium is the major cause of incapacity in general hospitals and other institutional settings, studies that examine decision-making capacity in hospital inpatients can generally be interpreted to reflect the impact of delirium (and/or dementia) on treatment consent capacity. Those studies are reviewed in the previous section.

One important empirical aspect of delirium and capacity is worth mentioning because it has implications for assessment. Although delirium is generally thought of as a dysfunction of cognitive abilities (such as attention, memory, visual–spatial, language, and other functions—thus the term "global" impairment), there are instances where prominent psychotic symptoms are present without a similar degree of cognitive impairment (Meagher et al., 2007). In a study of 100 consecutive patients on a palliative care service who exhibited delirium, 49 had symptoms of psychosis. They tended to be younger patients with more severe affect lability, and hallucinations and delusions tended to not be associated with cognitive disturbance (although another psychotic symptom— thought process disturbance—was closely correlated with attention, memory, orientation, and comprehension; Meagher et al., 2007). For these patients, brief cognitive screens (such as the MMSE [Folstein, Folstein, & McHugh, 1975]) may be misleading if the psychotic symptoms are relatively hidden (e.g., due to paranoid delusions) and the patient appears superficially intact cognitively. Indeed, incapacity in such patients can be very difficult to assess (see chapter 6 for a discussion of such an example).

DEMENTIA

Dementia is a general cognitive impairment that is chronic, usually in elderly people. A recent population-based study found that nearly 14% of adults over the age of 70 suffer from dementia in the United States. Of these, 74% have Alzheimer's disease (AD) and another 16% suffer from vascular dementia—the two most common causes of dementia (Plassman et al., 2007). Another 22% suffer from predementia states of cognitive impairment (Plassman et al., 2008). Because these are highly prevalent and chronic conditions, there are relatively many more studies that specifically examine the relationship between the dementias (most often AD) and consent capacity. Not unexpectedly, persons with dementia or cognitive impairment are more likely to be incompetent or have impaired decisional abilities than their older counterparts without these diagnoses of dementia or cognitive impairment (Bassett, 1999; Dymek, Atchison, Harrell, & Marson, 2001; Fazel, Hope, & Jacoby, 1999; Fitten & Waite, 1990; Kim, Caine, Currier, Leibovici, & Ryan, 2001; Marson, Annis, McInturff, Bartolucci, & Harrell, 1999; Marson, Earnst, Jamil, Bartolucci, & Harrell, 2000; Marson et al., 1995b; Stanley, Stanley, Guido, & Garvin, 1988; Wong, Clare, Holland, Watson, & Gunn, 2000) and than younger patients with schizophrenia (Wong et al., 2000).

However, it is worth noting that even among those with dementia (such as AD), there is sufficient heterogeneity such that one cannot simply equate dementia with incapacity. For example, in one study (Marson et al., 1995b), all patients with mild to moderate AD (mean MMSE = 19.4) were decisionally impaired (defined psychometrically as performing 2 SD below the mean score) on the understanding legal standard, yet 28–83% had adequate decisional abilities on the other relevant legal standards of appreciation, reasoning, or choice. Others have found that the quality of reasoning in patients with AD, and the comprehension of risks and benefits, was similar to that in elderly controls (Stanley et al., 1988). Two other studies reported that 34% of patients with mild to mild-moderate AD (mean MMSE 22.9) performed above a clinician panel-validated threshold on all four standards of decision-making ability (Kim et al., 2001), and 50% performed above the threshold for adequate ability on a measure of comprehension for advance directives (Bassett, 1999).

Nevertheless, despite the heterogeneity, the dementing illnesses in general have a major impact on consent capacity, even when the disease is in the early stages. In a recent study of 60 patients with Minimal Cognitive Impairment (MCI) with a mean MMSE score of 28.4 (on a 0–30 scale where 30 is a perfect score), 33% were marginal or below on a test of appreciation, 27% were marginal or below on reasoning, and 53% were marginal or below on the understanding standard. In this study, "marginal or below" was defined psychometrically as persons falling 1.5 *SD* below the control group mean (Okonkwo et al., 2007).

Another common finding in studies of persons with AD is that although subjects have significant difficulties with various components of the capacity interview, they tend to have little trouble expressing a preference and, further, their preferences are usually quite "reasonable." For example, even significantly impaired dementia patients, as a group, tend to make research participation choices that are similar to a normal control group's (Kim, Cox, & Caine, 2002a). In studies that elicit treatment consent capacity and treatment preferences, even patients with AD who perform quite poorly on measures of understanding, appreciation, and reasoning will in fact make treatment preference choices that are similar to what most people would in fact choose according to physician recommendations (Marson et al., 1995b). Of course, a "reasonable choice" is not one of the capacity standards, and these results should not be taken to mean that such patients retain capacity; but the results serve as a reminder that even incompetent patients retain some important abilities.

Finally, although the vast majority of capacity research has been conducted with persons with AD and related disorders, other neurodegenerative disorders with cognitive impairment will of course be associated with impaired decision-making abilities. For example, depending on the legal standard used, 25–80% of Parkinson's disease

3
chapter

INFO

Dementing illnesses generally have a major impact on consent capacity, although patients with milder degrees of dementia have capacity-related abilities that are more variable.

patients with "mild" level of cognitive impairment were found to be marginally capable or incapable (Dymek et al., 2001).

NEUROPSYCHOLOGICAL PREDICTORS OF IMPAIRED CAPACITY IN DEMENTIA

Understanding the neuropsychological underpinnings of decisional impairment is important for several reasons. It can provide construct validity to measures of decision-making abilities (Marson et al., 1995b), open the possibility of targeted interventions to enhance decision making (Christensen, Haroun, Schneiderman, & Jeste, 1995; Marson, Chatterjee, Ingram, & Harrell, 1996), and suggest supplementary tools for assessing decisional capacity (Bassett, 1999; Royall, 1994).

The most extensive theoretical and empirical effort toward building a "neurological model of incompetence" is the work of Marson and colleagues. Multiple cognitive functions seem to account for impaired decision-making abilities in patients with AD, but one consistent theme is the importance of *executive functions*. Executive functions are cognitive functions that "orchestrate relatively simple ideas, movements, or actions into complex goal directed behavior" (Royall et al., 1997). Bedside assessment methods (Royall, Mahurin, & Gray, 1992) and neuropsychological tests such as Trails A (Bassett, 1999), word fluency (Marson, Cody, Ingram, & Harrell, 1995a), and tests of conceptualization (Marson et al., 1996) that measure aspects of executive function predict impairments in decisional abilities. A qualitative analysis of error behaviors of patients with AD also supports the link between executive function and decisional abilities (Marson et al., 1999).

Factor analysis reveals that decision-making capacity seems to involve two broad domains: verbal reasoning/conceptualization and verbal memory (Dymek, Marson, & Harrell, 1999). Neuropsychological measures of conceptualization, executive function, language/semantic memory, and attention are correlated with the reasoning/conceptualization factor, whereas measures of immediate and delayed verbal recall are closely related to the verbal memory factor (Dymek et al., 1999).

Psychotic Disorders

The influence of psychotic disorders on treatment consent capacity has been extensively studied over the past three decades. Indeed, the decisional abilities of persons with schizophrenia and related disorders have been studied more extensively than probably for any other group of patients. Appelbaum and Grisso provide an excellent comprehensive review of the empirical literature on consent capacity research up to 1995 (Appelbaum & Grisso, 1995; Grisso et al., 1995). The following discussion combines that review as well as subsequent data. Virtually all of the research to date can be summarized by three main points.

CHRONIC PSYCHOSIS IS A RISK FACTOR FOR INCAPACITY

First, chronic psychotic disorders are a risk factor for impaired consent capacity. But because of heterogeneity within the group, one cannot infer incapacity from a diagnosis. Despite methodological heterogeneity, even the earliest studies found impaired understanding in persons with schizophrenia as a group (Benson, Roth, Appelbaum, Lidz, & Winslade, 1988; Grossman & Summers, 1980; Irwin et al., 1985; Munetz & Roth, 1985; Roth et al., 1982; Schachter, Kleinman, Prendergast, Remington, & Schertzer, 1994).

The best and most comprehensive study to date is the MacArthur Treatment Competence Study published in 1995, a multicenter study involving 498 subjects using lengthy and detailed instruments (Grisso & Appelbaum, 1995). This study enrolled acutely ill, hospitalized patients with schizophrenia. Patients with schizophrenia performed worse than their normal counterparts on every aspect of consent capacity. For any given ability measure, about 25% of the persons with schizophrenia failed a psychometric threshold for capacity, with 52% of the persons with schizophrenia failing at least one measure (Grisso & Appelbaum, 1995). An important implication of that research is that there is no empirically verifiable hierarchy of stringency among the abilities to understand, appreciate, and reason, as has been asserted by some (Drane, 1984). These results have been largely replicated using a shorter, more user-friendly instrument called the MacCAT-T (Grisso et al., 1997; Vollmann, Bauer, Danker-Hopfe, & Helmchen, 2003).

Although there is unequivocal evidence for impaired consent capacity in persons with chronic psychoses as a group, there is tremendous heterogeneity within that group. At one extreme, it is clear that a significant minority of patients with chronic psychotic disorders are seriously impaired. Some of these patients are even excluded from enrollment in capacity studies by clinicians who feel they are too impaired even for the interview study (Grisso & Appelbaum, 1995). Even among eligible patients for capacity studies such as the MacArthur studies, about 10% were unable to finish the interviews due to agitation (Grisso & Appelbaum, 1995; Grisso et al., 1997). Nevertheless, among acutely ill psychotic patients with symptoms severe enough for psychiatric inpatient admission, nearly half of those who were able to cooperate with the capacity interview performed adequately on all the subscales relevant to consent capacity.

Among stable outpatients in assisted living, the performance is even better. In a recent study comparing 59 relatively older (mean age 50.2) patients with schizophrenia with control subjects (Palmer, Dunn, Appelbaum, & Jeste, 2004), only the measure of understanding showed a significant difference between controls and patients, and on average the patient group performed quite well on that ability. Reasoning and expression of choice were similar between the two groups. The mean appreciation score was 3.5 (scale 0–4) for the patients (controls were not given the task, given that the questions probe insight into having schizophrenia; Palmer et al., 2004). Overall, the performance of these more stable outpatients with chronic psychotic disorders on the standard measures of consent capacity were quite good, despite their older age.

INCAPACITY IS USUALLY DUE TO COGNITIVE SYMPTOMS
Second, the main summary point about the relationship between chronic psychoses and consent capacity is that performance on abilities related to consent capacity is more a function of cognitive symptoms (and negative symptoms) than of classic positive psychotic symptoms (Palmer & Savla, 2007). Studies suggest that patients' performance is correlated only modestly with psychotic symptoms and more strongly with cognitive dysfunction (Carpenter

et al., 2000). Others have found that cognitive symptoms and negative and disorganized symptoms correlate with consent capacity, whereas positive symptoms do not (Moser et al., 2002). The correlations with various cognitive tests seem to exist without a clear pattern of connection between particular cognitive domains and consent capacity (Palmer et al., 2004; Saks et al., 2002). Palmer et al. note that these findings are consistent with the established link between neuropsychological performance (rather than severity of psychopathology) and everyday functioning (Palmer & Savla, 2007).

In studies my colleagues and I have conducted, when we qualitatively coded the error behaviors of persons with schizophrenia stable enough to cooperate with capacity interviews, we found that negative-type symptoms tend to distinguish the patient group from the normal controls, with very few occurrences of positive symptoms such as delusions and hallucinations interfering with the patients' decision-making abilities (Kim, unpublished data).

In total, these data suggest that decisional incapacity in persons with chronic psychotic disorders is best conceptualized as reflecting brain dysfunction resulting in cognitive impairment, more than a direct by-product of positive symptoms of psychosis such as hallucinations and delusions. In fact, the best predictor of capacity status is probably the overall level of independent functioning that the patient exhibits. Such information may be quite valuable in framing the prior probability estimates of incapacity.

INTERVENTIONS CAN IMPROVE UNDERSTANDING

Third, several studies have shown that understanding of factual information can be improved through interventions in persons with chronic psychotic disorders. In one study, an educational session using a slide presentation for older, chronically psychotic individuals and normal controls showed that the patient group performed worse than the controls in a comprehension test, but the patient group who received enhanced explanation of consent information showed comprehension similar to the normal group (Dunn et al., 2002).

BEST PRACTICE

Gather evidence regarding the patient's baseline everyday functioning and about whether the patient has undergone any recent deterioration.

Others have shown that brief "remediation" sessions (going over the informed consent materials) tend to improve patients' understanding performance to the point that it becomes comparable to a normal control group's (Carpenter et al., 2000), or that a 15-min education session seems to lead to higher performance (Moser et al., 2002).

Other studies have provided further evidence that at least factual comprehension can be improved with a variety of interventions in persons with schizophrenia (Stiles, Poythress, Hall, Falkenbach, & Williams, 2001; Wirshing, Wirshing, Marder, Liberman, & Mintz, 1998; Wong et al., 2000). Few data exist, however, on the effects on other consent capacity-related abilities like appreciation and reasoning. Still, from a practical perspective, the fact that interventions in general can improve the performance of these patients is highly significant, as it suggests that a capacity evaluator should ensure that conditions for performance are optimized, for example, through repeated discussions. This point will be revisited in chapter 5 when discussing the process of performing consent capacity evaluations.

Mood Disorders

MANIA

A manic episode, a hallmark of bipolar disorder (sometimes called manic depressive illness), is accompanied by several of the following symptoms: impulsivity, grandiose thinking, distractibility, rapid speech and "racing thoughts," increased activity, and lack of the need for sleep. It is often accompanied by frank psychotic beliefs and poor judgment in personal interactions, in spending money, and in risky activity. It is not difficult to see why such a constellation of symptoms would pose questions about informed consent, because the manic patient has difficulty controlling his thoughts and impulses, and his "valuing" ability (i.e., the ability to find things, persons, and activities meaningful and important) is often dramatically impaired.

A recent study examined manic patients' ability to provide consent for research (Misra, Socherman, Park, Hauser, & Ganzini,

2008). The researchers used a 11-item understanding instrument, and disclosure and testing were repeated twice. Manic patients performed worse than did nonmanic bipolar patients on the first trial, but by the third attempt, there were no significant differences between the groups in understanding (Misra et al., 2008). Appreciation and reasoning abilities were not assessed—domains which, given the nature of the illness, may be more relevant.

In contrast, a recent British study found that virtually all (97%) patients admitted to a psychiatric unit in a manic state were deemed to be incapable of making a treatment decision (either for medications or for psychiatric admissions; Owen et al., 2008). The study generally focused on the prevalence of incapacity in psychiatric inpatient units and did not provide further data about those manic patients.

Finally, another study from the United Kingdom found that 62% of acutely manic patients admitted to a psychiatric unit lacked capacity to consent to treatment, based on a clinical assessment of capacity (Beckett & Chaplin, 2006). More severe the manic state, more likely the patient was incapacitated; whereas higher IQ predicted lower likelihood of incapacity.

In summary, mania is a significant risk factor for incapacity, although the ability to understand may be amenable to interventions. Fortunately, manic states are often brief (at least in comparison to the symptomatic states in schizophrenia or depression) and there are effective treatments for mania. Thus, if at all possible, the capacity evaluator should attempt to treat and return the patient to a more stable state as a matter of first priority.

DEPRESSION

In contrast to the relatively few research studies on mania and capacity, there have been numerous studies on the effect of depression on consent capacity. Mild to moderate depression has little effect on the abilities relevant to consent capacity (Appelbaum, Grisso, Frank, O'Donnell, & Kupfer, 1999; Stiles et al., 2001; Vollmann et al., 2003). Even acutely ill, hospitalized patients with depression tend to perform fairly well. In a study of 92 acutely ill, hospitalized depressed patients with mean Beck Depression

Inventory scores of 30 (*SD* 11.4; Grisso & Appelbaum, 1995), only 5.4% had impaired understanding, 7.6% had impaired reasoning, and 11.9% had impaired appreciation. Given that the cutoff scores for "impairment" were based on scores that defined the bottom 5% of community controls, this study shows that hospitalized depressed patients, despite the level of depressive symptoms present, performed only slightly worse than the control group.

What about the very sickest of the depressed patients—for example, those being evaluated for electroconvulsive therapy (ECT)? In one study, after excluding patients with MMSE scores of 20 or lower and patients with legally incompetent status, researchers studied 40 patients about to undergo ECT treatment for severe depression (Lapid et al., 2003). The primary focus of the study was comparing two types of education for informed consent. Although there were no differences in effect between the two education interventions, intervention per se increased performance levels on the MacCAT-T such that the standard intervention group's final scores on measures of abilities relevant to capacity were near maximum range. Of the 40 subjects, 11 had symptoms consistent with psychotic depression. These patients had significantly worse performance on the Appreciation subscale of the MacCAT-T both pre- and postintervention. Although this study did not have a control group, based on the absolute scores, the authors concluded that "most patients with severe depression who require ECT appear to have decisional capacity to give informed consent to treatment" (Lapid et al., 2003). However, it is important to remember that this conclusion does not apply to those excluded from the study, namely, those ECT-eligible depressed patients who were already legally incompetent before the development of the depressive episode or those who were excluded because they already had significant cognitive impairment.

Another study examined 96 psychiatric inpatients referred for ECT whose medical records revealed that 21 of them had been deemed incompetent to make treatment decisions (Bean, Nishisato, Rector, & Glancy, 1994). Not enough clinical data are given to make a reliable comparison between the Bean et al. study and the Lapid et al. study. But once the exclusion criteria of the Lapid et al. study are taken into account, the two studies seem fairly congruent. It is likely that a significant minority of persons depressed enough to receive ECT lack treatment consent capacity. However, majority of patients with even severe depression (without dementia or psychosis) probably retain their capacity to consent to treatments such as ECT.

Traumatic Brain Injury (TBI)

According to the Centers for Disease Control, an estimated 5.3 million Americans (just over 2% of the population) live with disabilities resulting from TBI (National Center for Injury Prevention and Control, 2009). The annual societal cost of TBI is estimated to be $48.3 billion. The leading causes of TBI are falls, motor vehicle accidents, moving injuries (such as from sports), and assaults. The number of TBI patients seeking services has increased, as survival rates have increased due to improved head trauma care. The issue of decision-making capacity looms large in the brain injury rehabilitation setting (Marson et al., 2005; Mukherjee & McDonough, 2006). With the ever increasing number of combat veterans who survive TBIs, it is likely that the issue of TBI and treatment consent capacity will become even more important in the years to come.

TBI-related impairment poses a characteristic problem in that the issue of frontal lobe injury with attendant loss of executive functioning becomes a major issue in the assessment of consent capacity (Reid-Proctor, Galin, & Cumming, 2001). As noted above, executive functions refer to cognitive control functions that "orchestrate relatively simple ideas, movements, or actions into complex, goal-directed behavior" (Royall et al., 1997). The boundaries are not as clear for other brain functions (such as memory, motor function, smell), but the basic idea is the set of brain processes that are necessary to coordinate one's thoughts and actions to comport with one's goals and motives. Much of this function is thought to reside in the frontal lobes—unfortunately a very common site of brain injury (Reid-Proctor et al., 2001).

Studies have shown that executive dysfunctions are associated with decreased consent-related abilities in medical and neurologic patients (Holzer, Gansler, Moczynski, & Folstein, 1997; Marson

et al., 1996; Royall et al., 1997). But from the capacity evaluators' standpoint, the problem is that executive dysfunctions are
often difficult to measure without formal neuropsychological evaluation (Reid-Proctor et al., 2001). Also, for patients with executive dysfunction but relatively preserved language, social skills, and
memory, the typical clinical interview will fail to detect the degree
of functional impairment that the person may exhibit outside the
hospital. Evaluation of such patients requires corroborating evidence regarding events and behavior outside the hospital.

In terms of studies specifically aimed at understanding the
consent capacity-related abilities of persons with TBI, there has
been only one well-designed empirical study. In a study of 24
moderate to severe patients with TBI, the patients at the end of
their acute care hospitalization showed, in comparison to matched
controls, significantly decreased ability to appreciate, reason, and
understand (Marson et al., 2005). These impairments did improve
over the course of the subsequent 6 months, although the patients
continued to do worse than the controls. It is notable that in their
sample of 24 patients with moderate to severe TBI, 6 months after
acute hospitalization 25% were marginally capable or incapable in
terms of their appreciation ability and 34% were marginally capable
or incapable in terms of their understanding (based on a psychometric criterion of 1.5 SD below the mean of control performance;
Marson et al., 2005).

Mental Retardation

Children with mental retardation (MR) are presumed incompetent
just as all children are, as a matter of legal status. However, for adults
with MR, depending on the severity of impairment, their treatment
consent capacity varies considerably. In one study that compared
mild MR (IQ 55–80) and moderate MR (IQ 36–54) adults with
non-MR controls on treatment consent capacity for low-risk elec-
tive treatment procedures, most mild MR adults' understanding
and choice abilities were similar to that of controls, but mild MR
adults were significantly more impaired than controls on the appreciation and reasoning abilities (Cea & Fisher, 2003). Although
about half of the moderate MR adults were able to communicate

a choice, they tended to do quite poorly on the other abilities (Cea & Fisher, 2003). In another study by the same authors with a similar subject sample and focusing this time on research consent capacity, 18–68% of mild MR and 4–34% of moderate MR adults performed in the range of the normal subjects (depending on the domain of understanding examined). Appreciation performance was better (for mild MR group, 74–92% were within normal range) but the reasoning performance was much worse (Fisher, Cea, Davidson, & Fried, 2006).

One study compared persons with chronic psychoses, dementia, and MR (Wong et al., 2000). The psychosis group's Brief Psychiatric Rating Scale mean score was 40.1(*SD* 10.6; consistent with inpatient level of severity), the MR group had a verbal IQ mean of 60.2 (*SD* 8.8), and the dementia group had an MMSE mean of 11.9 (*SD* 5.2). Using a semistructured measure for capacity, the authors determined incapacity rates of 10% among psychotic patients, of 35% among the MR group, and of 67% among the dementia group, for a very low-risk procedure (Wong et al., 2000).

Substance Use Disorders

Although most states make provisions for a possible conservator-ship when substance-abusing persons show evidence of significant functional impairment (Rosen & Rosenheck, 1999), very little empirical data exist regarding treatment consent capacity and substance use disorders. In this diagnostic domain, the question of decision-making authority is raised far less commonly than questions about the ability to maintain a desired pattern of behavior over time (Hazelton, Sterns, & Chisholm, 2003; Rosen & Rosenheck, 1999). So for example, a nonintoxicated person with a substance use disorder with a long history of repeated episodes of poor self-care resulting from substance use will likely perform quite well on a typical treatment consent capacity interview (unless there are other issues, such as dementia due to substance use) but may not be able to remain sober enough to safely care for herself in the long run. By usual criteria for treatment consent capacity, such persons would be considered to have intact capacity. Thus it is not surprising that no studies seem to have been done to examine treatment consent capacity in this population, although there are numerous theoretical analyses (Charland, 2002), medico-legal analyses (Cohen, 2002), or case vignettes (Hazelton et al., 2003).

Other Conditions

In clinical experience, one does encounter cases in which conditions such as personality disorders or excessive anxiety raise questions of impaired consent capacity. But there are no systematic studies examining these issues. Medical conditions that do not directly impair cognitive functions generally have not been shown to affect abilities relevant to treatment consent, including cardiac illness (Appelbaum & Grisso, 1997), diabetes mellitus (Palmer et al., 2005), and HIV infection (as long as there is no additional cognitive impairment; Moser et al., 2002). One study of ambulatory cancer patients showed that significant impairment in understanding for research consent may occur in this population, but most of this seems to be explained by cognitive dysfunction, age, and education (the study sample contained a relative high proportion of persons without a high school diploma, 40%; Casarett, Karlawish, & Hirschman, 2003).

Anorexia nervosa has engendered an interesting debate regarding how best to determine the competence status in these patients (Grisso & Appelbaum, 2006; Tan, Stewart, Fitzpatrick, & Hope, 2006). In a small quantitative and qualitative study of 10 young women (and girls) assessing whether they were competent to refuse treatment of anorexia nervosa, the authors found that although the subjects showed "excellent understanding, reasoning, and ability to express choice," two subjects showed deficiency in appreciation (either ambivalent in belief about one's diagnosis or flat denial of it; Tan et al., 2006). This is of course not unexpected, because one of the diagnostic criteria for anorexia in the Diagnostic and Statistics Manual of Mental Disorders (Fourth Edition) (DSM-IV) is "[d]isturbance in the way in which one's body weight or shape is experienced, undue influence of body weight or shape on self-evaluation, or denial of the seriousness of the current low body weight." Beliefs based on the distorted self-perception or denial of the consequences of seriously low body weight may indicate loss of appreciation.

Use of Cognitive Tests and Efficacy of Interventions

How Useful Are Cognitive Tests in Predicting Incapacity?

Cognitive tests cannot be used as a stand-in for a specific capacity assessment. The patient's capacity to make the treatment decision at issue must be evaluated directly. However, brief cognitive tests can be useful aids in the overall capacity evaluation in a couple of ways. First, they can help establish that cognitive impairment indeed exists, and provide a sense of the degree of cognitive impairment. Given that delirium and dementia often may not be noticed by busy clinicians when the patients have sufficiently intact language and social abilities, such tests can be useful. It is not unusual for a consult to be triggered because the treatment team is concerned about a patient's refusal of a treatment, only to discover that underlying the refusal is a profound degree of cognitive impairment that becomes apparent only on targeted examination.

Second, to the extent that research data show that a given degree of impairment predicts decisional incapacity (for a given risk–benefit situation), such data may be useful for establishing predictive values of capacity determinations. An obvious caveat is that data on the relationship between cognitive tests and consent capacity are most relevant for those causes of incapacity that involve cognitive dysfunction (rather than for psychotic symptoms such as delusions).

The MMSE (Folstein et al., 1975) is perhaps the most well-known bedside cognitive screen. Because it is so widely known and used, the remainder of this section discusses the utility of the MMSE in a capacity assessment.

Although the MMSE score can be useful, one cannot assume that there is a simple relationship between MMSE performance and capacity. A normal score on the MMSE may sometimes be compatible with incapacity (Schindler, Ramchandani, Matthews, & Podell, 1995) whereas a low MMSE score can be compatible with good performance on some comprehension measures (Janofsky, McCarthy, & Folstein, 1992). Some have found that, for example, in a sample of

20 AD subjects, the MMSE (mean score of 22.0, *SD* 4.1) was not a useful estimator of a patient's decisional impairment (Bassett, 1999).

How then might MMSE be useful in capacity evaluations? The most fruitful way of using the MMSE scores is to categorize the scores into three domains with two cutoff scores: a lower cutoff (probably somewhere around 16–18) score and an upper cutoff score (around 24–26). A study of general hospital patients found optimal cutoff scores in using 16 or below for predicting incapacity, and 24 or above for predicting capacity (Etchells et al., 1999). A study of nursing home residents found that using MMSE cutoff scores of 18 and 26 best predicted incapacity and capacity, respectively (Pruchno et al., 1995). In a study of patients with AD, MMSE scores of 21–25 were surprisingly uninformative in predicting the capacity status of these patients, although scores below and above were quite predictive of these patients' capacity status (Kim & Caine, 2002). Thus, the utility of the MMSE depends on the context and the use to which it is put. Because the test is so routinely obtained, the utility gained comes at virtually no extra cost or effort.

It is possible that at dementia specialty clinics and research centers where simple neuropsychological tests—such as the Trails A test (Bassett, 1999) or word fluency measures (Marson et al., 1995a; Marson et al., 1996)—are routinely performed, they might serve or even surpass the function we describe here for the MMSE. From a practical perspective, this is an important area for further study.

Improving Consent Capacity with Education and Remediation?

We have already discussed earlier in this chapter the strong body of evidence that educational interventions can improve comprehension in persons with bipolar disorder (even in a manic state; Misra et al., 2008) and schizophrenia (Carpenter et al., 2000; Dunn, Lindamer, Palmer, Schneiderman, & Jeste, 2001; Stiles et al., 2001; Wirshing et al., 1998). It would appear that as long as the neuropsychiatric impairment does not severely impair the ability to learn itself, there is the hope of improving the patient's treatment consent capacity, or at least the understanding component. Of course, these considerations again apply to impairments that are due to cognitive dysfunction rather than, for example, psychotic delusions.

Can interventions help in the elderly population at risk for incapacity? In normal elderly volunteers, various types of interventions improve comprehension (Taub & Baker, 1983; Taub, Kline, & Baker, 1981). In a study of 34 elderly residents of a long-term care facility (MMSE 26.9 ± 2.5), an educational intervention enhanced understanding of a hypothetical treatment in the residential group as well as in a matched community dwelling group, although to a greater extent in the community dwellers (Krynski, Tymchuk, & Ouslander, 1994). A study of elderly medical inpatients (MMSE 26.7 ± 3.2) showed that the mode of disclosure of information affected understanding. Specifically, presenting information one part at a time rather than in an uninterrupted disclosure led to greater understanding (Grisso & Appelbaum, 1995; Dellasega, Frank, & Smyer, 1996). In a study of a slightly more impaired group of 54 elderly nursing home patients (MMSE 25.0 ± 3.2), a simplified disclosure format improved decision-making abilities—but only if 20 persons deemed to have dementia were not counted in the analysis (Tymchuk, Ouslander, & Rader, 1986). In a study of 53 more impaired geriatric medical inpatients with MMSE score of 22.9 ± 5.1, an interesting intervention of allowing the patients to go through a "1 week tryout" of a research study improved understanding of that study, even among the more impaired subgroup of patients with dementia (Rikkert, van den Bercken, ten Have, & Hoefnagels, 1997). Other studies involving persons with relatively mild stages of cognitive impairment or dementia have shown that repetition-based reinforcement of information may enhance understanding (Buckles et al. 2003; Mittal et al. 2007). However, studies involving persons with moderate to severe dementia, not surprisingly, are not as encouraging (Bourgeois, 1993; Wong et al., 2000).

INFO

Research supports the usefulness of educational interventions for incapacity; however, the outcome depends on the cause and severity of impairment.

These data suggest that interventions can improve the decisional abilities of cognitively impaired elderly persons, but the degree of benefit likely will depend on the type and severity of the impairment present. A person with very mild AD with memory deficits who retains the ability to stay on task (or can be easily helped to do so) may benefit from interventions. But as the disease progresses, the attempt to temporarily improve performance may be more a cosmetic exercise than a meaningful improvement.

What Do We Know About the Evaluators of Capacity?

There are several studies showing that the treating medical team tends to underestimate the consent capacity impairment of patients (Fitten et al., 1990; Raymont et al., 2004). For example, in one study, the treatment team identified as incompetent only 24% of those deemed incompetent by a more thorough, formal evaluation (Raymont et al., 2004). A nursing home study found that staff recognized only 13 of the 20 incompetent patients in the study sample as incompetent (Barton et al., 1996).

There are probably several reasons for this discrepancy. The treating team may employ a low threshold for competence when patients agree with the recommended treatment. Or it may be because the teams erroneously believe that as long as the patients "go along" with their recommendation, it is taken as evidence of intact capacity. On the other hand, if a patient accepts a recommended treatment that has clear benefits with little burden, the team may not be erring by using a low threshold for capacity. It could be that the researchers are using a threshold for capacity for a higher-risk decision (in general, these studies do not discuss the valence of the patient's decision, so it is not always clear what threshold was used in determining capacity).

But there may be other reasons why impairment tends not to be identified by treating teams. For example, patients with frontal lobe dysfunction sometimes have relatively intact language abilities, making it difficult to detect decisional deficits without more focused and in-depth examination or corroborating evidence (Schindler et al., 1995). To the extent that a treating team's failure to detect incapacity reflects a lack of awareness, rather than a thoughtful decision to allow the presumption of capacity to stand, there is a danger of inadequate informed consent.

Surveys have shown that health care professionals more familiar with capacity assessments, and who conduct formal capacity evaluations, report that other health care providers who call on them for consultations are poorly informed about the nature of treatment consent capacity. In a survey of CL psychiatrists, geriatricians, and geriatric psychologists, 22 of 23 "pitfalls" in assessment of consent capacity were rated as common by the majority of respondents (Ganzini, Volicer, Nelson, & Derse, 2003). These respondents were particularly concerned that general (nonpsychiatric) health care providers fail to understand the decision-specific nature of capacity judgments and that these providers also often fail to provide sufficient disclosure to patients when obtaining informed consent.

Yet mental health professionals may not do much better at capacity evaluations than general health care providers, according to some sources of evidence. One study from 1994 showed that even psychiatrists, who presumably receive more training than other physicians in capacity assessments, may fail to apply the correct criteria, or may apply them in a biased fashion, when evaluating treatment consent capacity (Markson, Kern, Annas, & Glantz, 1994). A survey conducted a decade later showed that almost a quarter of CL psychiatrists surveyed (as well as the same proportion of ethics committee chairs, geriatricians, and geriatric psychologists) wrongly identified as an essential criterion for competency that the patient "makes decision most other people would make" (Volicer & Ganzini, 2003). A UK study that was explicitly designed to test doctors' ability to conduct capacity assessments found that their subjects (ranging from preclinical medical students to senior psychiatrists) scored on average 25.1 out of 46 possible points on their test, with the psychiatrists doing not that much better than the rest (Whyte, Jacoby, & Hope, 2004).

Capacity evaluators themselves, when presented with "gray zone" cases, not surprisingly tend to disagree on their judgments. One study examined the capacity judgments of five physicians from different backgrounds (geriatric psychiatry, geriatric medicine, and neurology) who were asked to rate videotapes of capacity interviews of patients with mild AD and normal controls (Marson, McInturff, Hawkins, Bartolucci, & Harrell, 1997). The study found that the physicians' judgments of capacity for the patient group achieved overall agreement of only 56%, with a low group kappa statistic (.14) indicative of low agreement. These physicians, however, were able to significantly improve their agreement when directed to make their judgments using more explicit, narrowly defined individual legal standards (such as when explicit definitions of understanding and appreciation are used). Such a strategy not only resulted in greater agreement for each legal standard-based judgment (average of 76% agreement) but also in the overall global judgments of competence for each AD subject (Marson et al., 2000). Other studies have found that when physicians from the same discipline (psychiatry) use audio or audiovisual sources of information to make their judgments, the agreement tends to be much higher (Karlawish, Casarett, James, Xie, & Kim, 2005; Kim et al., 2001; Kim et al., 2007).

The variability among capacity evaluators probably has several causes. First, given that there is an inevitable judgment component, cases in the "gray zone" will create considerable variability. This inherent variability is probably unavoidable for some cases. Second, capacity evaluators may receive suboptimal training. In a survey that my colleagues and I conducted (Kim, Caine, Swan, & Appelbaum, 2006), we recruited CL psychiatrists from the Academy of Psychosomatic Medicine (the main professional organization for American and Canadian CL psychiatrists) membership list and found that the average number of lectures on assessment of capacity that these psychiatrists received during their training was 2.6, and the number of supervised cases was only just over 3. On average, these psychiatrists rated the quality of their training in capacity assessments as between "adequate" and "good" with an average of 2.5

INFO

For "gray zone" cases, there is considerable variability in judgments even among capacity evaluators who are mental health professionals.

on a 4-point scale—not a strong endorsement. Admittedly, this was a self-selected sample we employed for an experimental study, rather than a representative sample. But anecdotal experience is consistent with these findings.

Another source of variability among capacity evaluators seems to be related to their individual "styles" of focusing on particular types of deficits as indicative of impairment. In a study of physicians as competency evaluators of persons with AD (Marson, Hawkins, McInturff, & Harrell, 1997), those physicians who tended to be stringent (i.e., greater tendency to see an impaired AD patient as incapable) appeared to focus on short-term memory deficits. Because memory impairment occurs very early in AD, capacity evaluators who see such impairment as indicative of incapacity will appear more "strict" in their judgments. In contrast, the more "liberal" physicians seemed influenced by losses in simple executive functions—symptoms that may occur somewhat later in the course of the disease (Marson et al., 1997; Earnst, Marson, & Harrell, 2000). The issue of how capacity evaluators make their judgments is discussed further in chapter 6, in the context of interpreting interview data.

Instruments for Assessing Treatment Consent Capacity

Numerous instruments have been used to assess the abilities relevant to consent capacity, either for treatment decisions or for research participation decisions. Indeed, most research groups tend to use their own instruments for measuring abilities relevant to consent capacity (Kim et al., 2002b). This raises considerable problems in interpretation (see "Notes on Reading the Literature" section). A detailed examination of the variety of instruments is beyond the scope of this book but a reasonably comprehensive list is provided in Table 3.1 for reference. It provides a list of instruments used to measure one or more abilities relevant to either treatment consent capacity or research consent capacity. The reader is referred to the original articles and to three review sources for further discussions of these instruments. First, a chapter by

Table 3.1 | Instruments for Assessing Abilities Underlying the Capacity to Provide Informed Consent to Treatment or Research

Author and year	Name[a]	Research (R) or treatment (T) consent	Reviewed in (1) Dunn et al. (2006), (2) Moye (2003), and (3) Kim et al. (2002)
Appelbaum and Grisso (2001)	MacArthur Competence Assessment Tool—Clinical Research (MacCAT-CR)	R	1, 2
Bean et al. (1994)	Competency Interview Schedule	T	1
Buckles et al. (2003)	Brief Informed Consent Test	R	1
Carney, Neugroschl, Morrison, Marin, and Siu, (2001)	Competence Assessment Tool	T	3
Cea and Fisher (2003)	Assessment of Consent Capacity for Treatment	T	1
DeRenzo, Conley, and Love (1998)	Evaluation to Sign Consent	R	1
Draper and Dawson (1990)	Ontario Competency Questionnaire	T	1
Edelstein (1999)	Hopemont Capacity Assessment Interview	T	1, 2

(Continued)

Table 3.1 | (Continued)

Etchells et al. (1999)	Aid to Capacity Evaluation	T	1, 3
Fazel et al. (1999)	Vignette based	T as advance directive	3
Fitten et al. (1990)	Vignette based	T	1, 3
Grisso et al. (1995)	Understanding Treatment Disclosures	T	1, 2
Grisso et al. (1995)	Perception of Disorder	T	1, 2
Grisso et al. (1995)	Thinking Rationally about Treatment	T	1, 2
Grisso et al. (1997)	MacArthur Competence Assessment Tool— Treatment (MacCAT-T)	T	1, 2
Janofsky et al. (1992)	Hopkins Competency Assessment Test	T	1, 2
Marson et al. (1995b)	Capacity to Consent to Treatment Instrument	T	1, 2, 3
Miller, O'Donnell, Searight, and Barbarash (1996)	Deaconess Informed Consent Comprehension Test	R	1
Sachs et al. (1994)	Vignette-based instrument	R	1, 3

(Continued)

Table 3.1 | (Continued)

Author and year	Name[a]	Research (R) or treatment (T) consent	Reviewed in (1) Dunn et al. (2006), (2) Moye (2003), and (3) Kim et al. (2002)
Saks et al. (2002)	California Scale of Appreciation	R	1
Schmand, Gouwenberg, Smit, and Jonker (1999)	No specific name	T	1, 3
Stanley, Guido, Stanley, and Shortell (1984)	Competency Assessment Interview	R	1
Stanley et al. (1988)	No specific name	T	1, 3
Tymchuk et al. (1986)	25-Item True–False test	T	3
Vellinga, Smit, van Leeuwen, van Tilburg, and Jonker (2004)	Vignette- or actual decision-based structured interview	T	1
Wirshing et al. (1998)	Informed Consent Survey	R	1
Wong et al. (2000)	Decision assessment measure	T (diagnostic procedure)	3

[a] Not all instruments have author designated names and in such cases, a brief description is used.

Moye (2003) provides an in-depth, rigorous scientific review of six instruments listed in Table 3.1. Second, an article by Dunn et al. (2006) provides a more brief review of most of the instruments in

Table 3.1. Finally, Kim et al. discuss key issues in evaluating such instruments (2002b).

Should such instruments be used routinely in practice? If so, what are the critical issues in choosing one? Most of the instruments listed are not appropriate for routine use, for a variety of reasons that are explored as part of a chapter 5 discussion on how to assess abilities relevant to consent capacity. However, in chapter 5, two of the most widely cited instruments will be discussed and compared in some detail.

Notes on Reading the Research Literature

The quality of research on consent capacity continues to improve. But it is still a relatively small and new field of research, so there tends to be considerable heterogeneity in method and quality. It is important to keep in mind some of the complexities in interpreting capacity research reports. Following are a few key issues.

Consent Capacity Construct

First, most research groups tend to develop their own instrument for measuring the consent capacity-related abilities (Kim et al., 2002b). Unfortunately, the consent capacity construct, and the methods used to operationalize it, vary among studies. Because constructs vary between jurisdictions (Grisso & Appelbaum, 1998), and because commission reports and scholars vary in their descriptions of these constructs (Buchanan & Brock, 1989; President's Commission, 1982; Roth et al., 1977), this may not be surprising. But the variability among studies goes beyond these differences. Indeed, some studies do not elaborate a construct. And some studies use an unpublished instrument that is described in ways that make it difficult to assess the construct behind it, whereas other studies refer to the widely cited Appelbaum/Grisso four abilities model. Even in the latter cases, however, these instruments may be markedly different from each other, or just focus on one or two of the abilities, or, for example, operationalize the distinction between understanding and appreciation incorrectly.

Categorical Capacity Judgment

Second, beyond measuring the individual consent-related abilities (understanding, appreciation, reasoning), the issue of categorical capacity judgment in these research studies is problematic. (This issue of translating dimensional data on decisional abilities into categorical judgments about competence is discussed in much greater detail in chapter 6, as part of a discussion on interpretation of data.) There are of course no gold standards for categorical judgments, and researchers do a variety of things to arrive at a categorical judgment. This includes a purely statistical approach (e.g., assigning "incompetent" status to anyone who scores below a certain statistical cutoff, such as 2 SD below the mean of the patient group, or of a control group, if there is one). Another approach is an a priori cutoff based on intuitions of the researcher. Finally, the categorical status of a subject may be determined based on independent experts' categorical determinations. The latter method also varies considerably, as some studies use one expert reviewer whereas others use several. As one might imagine, the meaning of "incompetent" as defined by these three methods of translating dimensional data into categorical determinations of capacity may not necessarily overlap, and must be kept in mind in interpreting the studies.

Effect of Samples Studied

Third, the patient mix is important to consider when interpreting studies that claim that a certain method of assessment is valid and reliable in determining competence. For example, if a study's patient mix is bimodal—that is, consisting of high-functioning and low-functioning persons but relatively few in the middle—any method of discriminating incapable patients from capable patients will appear to be more effective than it actually is.

Summary

Treatment consent capacity assessments should be, as much as possible, evidence based. Because the field is still growing, and in many ways still developing in its methodology, the literature is often difficult to interpret. Although an attempt has been made in this chapter to provide a summary of valid and reliable results accumulated over the years, there are limitations to such studies that need to be kept in mind.

APPLICATION

Preparation for the Evaluation | 4

T he capacity evaluation process typically consists of the
following elements:

- The request for the consultation
- Gathering information before interview
- Interviewing staff, or others, as needed
- The interview with the patient
- Gathering further information, as needed
- Postevaluation tasks

These elements usually occur in the order listed, but may vary
depending on the case. This chapter focuses on the first three
elements (and gathering other information as needed), chapter 5
on the interview with the patient, and chapter 7 on post-evaluation
tasks.

The issues in preparation for a capacity evaluation vary considerably, depending on a variety of factors including the setting of the
evaluation, the nature of the need for a capacity evaluation, and the
availability of resources and expertise.

The Request for a Capacity Assessment

When is it appropriate or necessary to conduct a treatment consent
capacity evaluation? For the treatment team, there are two questions: Should this patient's treatment consent capacity be formally
assessed, or can the *presumption of capacity* stand? Should the
evaluation be conducted by a specialist or by a member of the
treating team?

Making the Referral to An Evaluator

All adults are presumed to be competent to make their medical decisions, and this doctrine is often an explicit part of statutes and policies. Thus, there needs to be some reason that suffices to put aside this presumption, at least enough to trigger a formal evaluation or a consultation. But there is no rule that can be applied to determine whether a formal evaluation ought to be done.

The need for a treatment consent capacity consultation most commonly arises, not surprisingly, in hospitals where major medical treatments take place. The issue arises more often in inpatient settings, but sometimes in outpatient clinics, for example, when planning a surgery or other treatments. In both settings, often physicians seek someone with special expertise to perform the evaluation. Urban centers, especially academic medical centers, have mental health specialists, such as CL professionals, and less often forensic psychiatrists or psychologists, with specialized training for performing capacity assessments.

The need for a mental health professional, such as a psychiatrist or a psychologist, to assess a patient's capacity also varies depending on the nature of the problem. This chapter, like the rest of the book, is written primarily for the mental health professional functioning as a consultant. However, in most states, there is no legal requirement that a capacity evaluation must be conducted by a specialist. (Although in some states, for special populations, such as patients with mental retardation, there is a requirement for an evaluation by a person with expertise in evaluating such persons.) Most statutes and policies refer to the "attending physician" or even just "physician." So from a legal point of view, there usually are no restrictions or special qualifications. If a member of the treating team has the time and the knowledge to perform a capacity evaluation, then there is some advantage because that person will be in the optimal position to convey the relevant medical facts to the patient, and will also have first-hand knowledge of the clinical—including cognitive and psychological—state of the patient. Indeed, when the patient is on a psychiatric service, the treating physician will be a psychiatrist who actually has considerable experience in determining treatment consent capacity and there will not be a need for a special consultant referral. However, on most nonpsychiatric units, given the increasing specialization in medicine, especially if the evaluation is not straightforward, it is common for mental health specialists to be consulted. Thus, the question of who conducts the evaluation is usually a matter of expertise and location rather than one of legal requirement.

Evaluating the Request for a Capacity Evaluation

An evaluation of a patient's consent capacity is more than just an interview with the patient. The evaluator must also assess the request for the consultation, gather relevant information prior to (and sometimes after) the patient interview, and perform key tasks following the evaluation. The evaluation begins from the moment of assessing the reason for, and the meaning of, the consultation. Any division of the evaluator's task as preparation to evaluation versus evaluation proper is therefore somewhat arbitrary.

The consultant should query those who are making the referral regarding their perception of the situation. Why does the referring team or physician think that the patient may be incapable? Such probing may reveal a range of reasons (Umapathy et al., 1999). Sometimes, the consultation is requested simply because the patient has a history of schizophrenia, without any specific behavioral or cognitive manifestations that worried the team. Or it may be because, despite a thorough and patient disclosure by the attending physician, the physician is not convinced that the patient is exhibiting sufficient understanding and would like a more detailed opinion. Sometimes the medical situation itself has features that require extra caution. For example, the treatment in question may be moderately beneficial but also very burdensome—a situation in which the treatment team would like to make sure the patient truly appreciates the trade-offs involved. Often the request arises after the patient has refused a treatment that the physician or treatment team believes is best for the patient. When a patient refuses a recommended treatment (or a diagnostic intervention) that could have significant consequences, it is not unreasonable to raise the question of whether the patient is fully capable of making the decision to refuse. But this point should not be confused with the paternalistic position, which takes a patient's disagreement as the basis for judging someone incompetent.

4
chapter

The true meaning of the consult may not become clear until well into the evaluation process. It may turn out that the problem is not so much a capacity evaluation issue but rather that a medical team is having difficulty managing a patient. This statement is not meant to denigrate the intentions or the competence of the treating team. It just means that the dynamics of some situations are difficult to recognize and to sort out, and that it is one of the tasks for the consultant. Mental health consultants such as consultation psychiatrists are familiar with the fact that the stated reason for a consultation is not always the real reason. Consider the following two types of situations.

A common scenario is a patient who refuses a recommended treatment or a diagnostic procedure:

> A 35-year-old HIV-positive man with a history of substance abuse
> and medication nonadherence is admitted to the hospital with
> pneumonia. The patient is refusing to cooperate with the team,
> refusing blood tests and other diagnostic procedures. The team
> asks, "Is he competent to refuse?"

Refusals from a patient are often an expression of anger, whether justified or not. If such a patient feels slighted or disrespected, he may assert his will by refusing what the team recommends, putting the team in a bind. The team may in turn become frustrated and unintentionally use the capacity evaluation as a kind of punishment or a threat. When an angry patient refuses a treatment that most patients would accept and creates havoc for the team, the consultant who barges in and pronounces the patient competent and leaves (assuming the patient is competent and the real issue is the management of a complicated patient) does not accomplish much and can make the situation worse. The best course to take is to first understand why the patient is refusing. The patient may feel slighted and helpless. It is not unusual for a patient with substance dependence or a personality disorder, or both, to have minimal coping capacity and behave in counterproductive ways. Such a consult request should be treated (at least initially) as a "difficult patient" management case (Groves, 1978). See also chapter 7.

Sometimes it is better to avert a capacity evaluation by changing the contextual factors in the patient's favor. The rule of thumb should be that if the patient will be served better with a solution that does not involve a capacity determination, then that is the better course to take. This seems too obvious to need pointing out but it is often forgotten. An example of this is an elderly patient, perhaps with mild dementia, who is at risk if she goes home by herself.

> An 80-year-old widow living in an assisted living apartment is admitted for congestive heart failure because she repeatedly forgets to take her medications. She has forgotten to turn the stove off and the fire department had to be called once. On clinical examination, she is determined to have mild dementia. She is adamantly refusing to consider a nursing home placement.

In such a case, it may indeed be true that the patient could put herself at risk and she may lack the insight to know this; she indeed may be incapable of making her own decision about living alone independently. However, it may well be true that if sufficient resources were available and provided, she may still be able to live in her own apartment for a longer time if the safety risks are reduced and a monitoring plan is implemented. Perhaps arrangements can be made for a reliable person to administer her medications every day. Perhaps she could stop using the stove (e.g., it could be disconnected so that she is unable to use it) and food could be delivered to her. Because the threshold for capacity must be adjusted to the potential consequences of the choices at hand, if the choice of the patient can be made safe enough, it may prove to be a better solution than forcing a capacity evaluation. Unfortunately, often the resources are lacking to provide such mitigation in risk, and a capacity evaluation may be necessary. But it is worth exploring whether a better outcome may be had by avoiding the evaluation altogether.

One could offer many more examples of how the request for a capacity evaluation may be addressed without the capacity evaluation being the central intervention. A creative clinical focus must be part of the capacity evaluator's outlook when evaluating a request for a capacity evaluation.

BEWARE
Part of the capacity evaluator's task is determining whether a capacity evaluation is indeed necessary (or sufficient); sometimes, a more clinically focused intervention may better serve the patient.

4
chapter

Finally, as the evaluator becomes familiar with each case, he should keep in mind whether the best course might be to focus on the patient's medical or psychiatric condition that is responsible for the impairment in decision making. Is it possible to treat the underlying condition, so that the evaluation becomes unnecessary? Must the decision regarding treatment be made that day? This is a basic reminder to the capacity evaluator to not take off the clinician's hat just because the consult has been labeled a "capacity consult." This point is particularly important when the treatment decision is irreversible, such as when a patient requests cessation of life-sustaining treatment.

Gathering Information Prior to Patient Interview

Understanding the Medical Situation

As we saw in chapter 2, capacity determination is not simply about patients' abilities but rather about their abilities in a particular context. One of the first tasks of the consultant is therefore to understand the patient's medical situation thoroughly enough to conduct a valid capacity evaluation. The ideal would be to have a conversation with the referring physician or a treatment team member to discuss the reasons for the consult. In eliciting the medical information, the consultant can simply use the domains that are required in informed consent disclosure. Thus the consultant will ask the physician to explain the patient's condition and prognosis, the proposed treatment (or diagnostic procedure) and its potential benefits and risks/discomforts, the alternatives to the proposed treatment and their potential benefits and risks/discomforts, and also what is likely to happen—the potential benefits and risks/discomforts— if no treatment is given. The consultant should also find out how much conversation has already taken place with the patient, including the nature and extent of the recommendation made by the treatment team. If the capacity evaluator is not a medical doctor, this conversation is even more important. All the necessary questions should be asked of the team to ensure that the evaluator will initiate the evaluation with a good handle on the facts.

Besides speaking with the team, the consultant should review any relevant current and past medical and psychiatric history (from old charts or electronic records), current neuroimaging studies, laboratory results, and recent and current medication lists. Because the very nature of capacity evaluations involves patients who have difficulty relaying their histories, this type of preparatory work will almost always be necessary. In addition, consultation notes from other medical services should be reviewed. Quite often in a tertiary care hospital, even the treatment team may not be the best source of medical information for a very specific medical situation. Thus, a direct conversation with the consultant in other specialties may be necessary. For some consultations, it may be useful to review or speak directly with others who have evaluated various functional capacities of the patient, such as occupational therapy and physical therapy services. Finally, although it is becoming rarer these days to find formal neuropsychological testing data, it should be reviewed whenever available.

BEST PRACTICE

In order to understand the patient's medical situation

- speak with the patient's medical team
- review the patient's medical and psychiatric history
- review lab results, medication lists, neuroimaging studies, and so on
- review consultation notes and/or speak directly with consultants
- review neuropsychological testing data if available

Gathering Information from Third Parties

Often it is essential to gather information from third parties. This could range from spouses, children, assisted living staff, staff at another facility (if the patient is a transfer from, for example, a state psychiatric hospital), and staff at the acute care hospital, among others. The type of information to be gathered varies as well. For example, a team may request a capacity evaluation regarding the patient's after-hospital disposition, based on reports of unsafe conditions at home. This will require some detective work by the consultant, often by speaking directly with persons outside the hospital who may have direct knowledge of the patient's functioning at home, which may indicate the nature of the patient's mental status changes over time, or the patient's prior stated wishes, or patterns of behavior that express her preferences regarding medical treatment.

Third-party information is obviously important when the patient is not able to give a reliable history, which is a very common situation with cognitively impaired patients. But it is also important in cases in which the patient's impairment is not obvious during an interview but the actual functioning may be quite impaired. Early dementia in a person with well-preserved language abilities (i.e., those functions that tend to make a patient "seem normal" in an interview), but with impaired executive function, will require a careful review of the patient's functioning outside the hospital to ascertain a sense of the true level of impairment (Schindler et al., 1995). A similar situation may occur in the case of a patient with traumatic brain injury whose primary deficit may be in executive functioning (Reid-Proctor et al., 2001). Such cases may require neuropsychological testing to establish the degree and domains of cognitive impairment to provide further objective evidence of impairment, in addition to careful interviews with third parties.

As helpful as third-party information may be, the capacity evaluator needs to follow some guidelines to optimize the quality of the information gathered and to carefully interpret the third-party information.

BEST PRACTICE

When gathering information from third parties, beware of potential informant bias. After initial open-ended questions, ask concrete and specific questions to gather facts with minimal interpretation by the informants.

First, the evaluator should have a sense of whether the third party may have interests that could color his information. A son who is frustrated by the stubborn refusals of an elderly widower father who, in the son's opinion, is "too old to take care of himself" may overinterpret the father's impairments, for example (Gutheil & Appelbaum, 2000, p. 219). Given the often emotionally charged circumstances, the evaluator needs to have a sense of where the informant is "coming from." This type of evaluation of the informant is important in the event of the patient being found incompetent and in need of a substitute decision maker.

Second, the accuracy of the information from third parties—especially from laypersons—will often depend on how concrete and specific the questions are. Thus, rather than accepting at face value "Oh, she's able to take care of herself fine," the evaluator might go down the list of details with questions like, "How many meals does she eat in a day? Who makes her breakfast? What does she eat? Does it require using the stove or the oven?" This is not to suggest that interviews with third parties forgo good interviewing practices, which include open-ended questions and allowing the interviewee to provide answers that one might not have expected. But the evaluator needs to have a clear idea of what he wants to find out from the source, and to phrase the questions in such a way that the answers provide concrete, reliable answers. For example, it is not unusual for a patient to be admitted with a story about some harm she has caused (or could have caused) due to her impairment. It is important to find out exactly what happened, what the circumstances were, and what the actual damage, if any, was. These stories can become either inflated or deflated as they are relayed from person to person, often depending on the incentives or bias of the person relaying the story. In such situations, the more concrete one can make the question, and less room for interpretation one gives the informant, the more accurate and reliable the information will be.

Gathering third-party information can take considerable amount of time and effort. The extra investment up-front is usually worth it, because the difficult, gray zone cases may get endlessly debated without solid corroborating data, costing even more time and delay.

Summary Checklist

By the time the evaluator is ready to enter the patient's room for an interview, he should have a fairly good grasp of items to explore, to

Table 4.1 | Checklist Prior to Patient Interview

- What exactly is the concern of those who are asking for the consultation? What is the (preliminary) evidence for their concern?
- What is the patient's medical condition, and what intervention is being proposed? What are the risks and benefits of the procedure, of the alternatives?
- What has the patient been told? Do I understand the medical situation well enough to provide the necessary informed consent disclosure for the purposes of conducting a capacity evaluation?
- What are the potential sources, causes, and severity of cognitive or psychiatric impairment, based on the information gathered so far? How should the interview be focused to confirm or disconfirm these hypotheses?
- What are some concrete, specific issues that must be raised with the patient (e.g., a statement she made, or questionable safety behavior)?

confirm, or to disconfirm. The questions in Table 4.1 may serve as a mental checklist. In general, the more information one has to provide a provisional framework for the evaluation, the better.

Data Collection—The Patient Interview | 5

In the assessment of treatment consent capacity, the patient interview will cover two main areas—the patient's clinical state and his specific abilities relevant to consent capacity. How should these two domains be assessed during the interview? If the capacity evaluator had plenty of time and cooperation from the patient, ideally one would perform a thorough clinical evaluation of the patient's neuropsychiatric condition before proceeding to a more focused capacity evaluation. A thorough mental status examination and some bedside cognitive tests will help focus and direct the capacity interview itself, because the evaluator will have a much better sense of the nature and degree of impairment, and the likely ways in which the patient may fail on one of the capacity standards. There is always the danger that jumping too early into the evaluation of the specific abilities could lead to ambiguous findings that are difficult to interpret without an overall clinical impression that could help explain the phenomena.

In the real world one often does not have the luxury of a thorough clinical interview with a detailed mental status examination preceding the capacity interview. Delirium is often accompanied by dysphoria and irritability, and a delirious patient's cooperation may not last long. Or a delusional, paranoid patient's patience may grow thin during a prolonged, probing evaluation. An early dementia patient who is trying to hide her deficits may refuse to cooperate further if she finds herself performing poorly on bedside cognitive tests. Thus, although in what follows the discussion is sequentially organized into a neuropsychiatric assessment and an assessment of the specific consent abilities, the evaluator will need to be flexible.

Assessing the Patient's Clinical Condition

Approaching the Patient

In approaching the patient for a capacity evaluation, it is worth considering the patient's point of view. Consider, for example, a patient on a general medical ward, one of the most common places for conducting a treatment consent capacity evaluation. A hospital room is, paradoxically, not an ideal place for an important interview such as a capacity assessment. If the patient has some type of cognitive or psychiatric impairment and is medically ill, he may be frightened, or perhaps just bewildered, in addition to not feeling well physically. For instance, he may have overheard, or been told directly, that there is a possibility of undergoing an operation that frightens him. There are many distracting noises, such as intravenous machines, various monitors, noises from the hallway, and the ubiquitous sound of the television set. There is also the lack of privacy (a roommate, and perhaps the roommate's visitors, engaged in conversation) with orderlies, phlebotomists, and other workers going in and out of the room, taking vital signs and removing meal trays. For a clinician who has become accustomed to such a setting, all of this is background noise, and it is easy to forget that a hospital room can be a less than ideal situation for peak interview performance for patients.

Thus it is imperative that the capacity evaluator remember, as much as possible, to arrange the setting to aid the patient. The TV should be turned off. Visitors should be asked to step outside, unless of course the patient prefers his family or friends to be present. (If so, they need to be told to only observe and not intervene to "help" the patient.) Any available means to increase privacy should be used (even if only curtains). The door should be closed, and other measures should be taken to ensure that a quiet, private, and uninterrupted environment is achieved.

Usually the evaluator will introduce herself as someone who is looking into the patients' ability to handle the treatment decision they need to make. When introducing oneself to the patient, there is no getting around the fact that patients do not initiate—and therefore do not expect—a capacity interview. It is always someone else's idea. Also, given that mental health professionals are the capacity evaluators in general hospitals, nonpsychiatric patients may wonder why an examination by a mental health professional is necessary. "I'm not crazy!" is not an unusual reaction. This potentially awkward situation is best addressed by simply and candidly stating the reason for the interview and explaining that the evaluator has been asked by the treatment team to see the patient.

Is a formal informed consent necessary for conducting the interview? Most experts would probably agree that an informal agreement and cooperation of the patient is sufficient. First, unlike other capacity determinations in which there is another party whose interests are also at stake (e.g., an employer or the government), the clinical capacity evaluation is primarily for the benefit of the patient—the aim is to balance the welfare and autonomy interests of the patient, rather than balancing the needs of the justice system with the interests of the patient (as would be in a court-directed forensic evaluation, for example). Indeed, this intent to help the patient in a broad sense should be part of the introductory rationale given to the patient to reassure him. Second, as others have noted (Grisso & Appelbaum, 1998), low-risk procedures such as a clinical interview during a hospital stay do not usually require separate informed consent.

Of course, patients do sometimes refuse capacity evaluations. An uncooperative patient complicates the evaluation in ways that are understandably anxiety provoking for the evaluator, because an important determination will have to be made with less than ideal information. But a systematic and thoughtful approach to such a situation is still possible, as will be discussed in chapter 6.

5
chapter

Assessment of Clinical Symptoms

The first step in the capacity evaluation is a clinical evaluation. It should be very similar to other clinical evaluations that a mental health clinician may perform. One obtains the history of current condition, past psychiatric and medical history, family history, social history, current medications, substance abuse history, and a review of pertinent laboratory and other studies. Any format that follows a similar outline would serve just as well.

Although much of the above may need to be obtained from the medical records or from collateral sources, especially if the patient is significantly impaired, there is much wisdom in gathering information in the standard clinical "workup" to provide the clinician a comfortable understanding of the case. This will ensure that a crucial piece of information is not inadvertently missed. Sometimes a piece of history (such as the death of a spouse a month prior to the patient's admission, and the social history to the effect that the spouse took care of the day-to-day running of the household) can explain the clinical picture of a patient who on interview appears to have a dementing condition but whose poor functioning had been hidden by the spouse, explaining the appearance of a "sudden" decline that is, after all, not so sudden. This will have clear implications, for example, on the reversibility of the patient's cognitive impairment, which in turn will have an impact on the overall management of the situation.

For the purposes of a capacity evaluation, it is useful to organize the kinds of impairment that can cause incapacity into two broad types. The first is cognitive dysfunction and is the most common reason found for incapacity in a general hospital. Cognitive dysfunctions include impairments in abilities such as attention, orientation, memory, language, visuospatial abilities, and executive function. The other category of symptoms is more often due to "psychiatric" conditions. This category includes psychotic symptoms (such as delusions, hallucinations, disorganized thinking, as well as negative symptoms such as lack of initiative), or symptoms of mania (distractibility, grandiosity, pressured speech, impulsivity, hyperactivity, and poor judgment), as well as other symptoms (anxiety or fear, dissociation, severe depressive symptoms,

BEST PRACTICE

Gather information to answer the following:

- Is there cognitive or other mental impairment?
- What is the nature of the impairment, such as its severity and the domains affected?
- What is the condition underlying the impairment?
- Is the condition reversible, or can the impairment be mitigated to enhance decision making?
- Is there a need for more formal testing, such as neuropsychological tests?

suicidality, rigid negativity, etc.). Of course, these are not diagnoses but descriptions of symptoms or impairments, and a given condition may manifest both cognitive and psychiatric symptoms. For example, delirium is ordinarily conceived of as an acute decline in global cognitive function but sometimes the more prominent cause of decisional impairment in a delirious patient may be her psychotic symptoms. On the other hand, what makes some persons with chronic psychoses, such as schizophrenia, incapable of providing treatment consent are not only the classic positive symptoms of delusions and hallucinations (although these can of course play an important role) but also (and perhaps more often) their general diminishment in cognitive function, as well as their negative symptoms (see chapter 3).

ASSESSING COGNITIVE SYMPTOMS

The cognitive dysfunctions should be assessed systematically, using brief bedside tests that the capacity evaluator is experienced in using. The most common screening test is the MMSE of Folstein et al. (1975). MMSE can be useful when one suspects cognitive dysfunction as the source of incapacity, and one needs to characterize the nature and severity of the impairment, which will in turn help guide and interpret the capacity interview per se. (See chapter 3 for a lengthier evidence-based discussion of the potential uses of tests such as the MMSE.)

5
chapter

Because MMSE is so widely used in general clinical evaluations, it is just as important to be familiar with its limitations in capacity evaluations. As noted earlier, the MMSE itself is not a capacity test. A very low score increases the likelihood of incapacity but does not justify by itself the judgment of incapacity. Further, perfect performance on any cognitive test does not rule out incapacity: A delusional patient, for example, may perform flawlessly on the MMSE but can be incompetent. And persons who may be incompetent due to impairment in executive function—that is, tasks that require higher-level, complex organizing of mental processes—may perform well on the MMSE.

BEWARE
Although important in capacity evaluations, the MMSE or other cognitive tests are not capacity tests per se; further capacity-specific information is needed to confirm either competency or incompetency.

When a patient performs reasonably well on the MMSE but the clinician feels that there are still undetected cognitive issues, then it is advisable to administer other bedside tests or tasks that the evaluator is comfortable using. These should target higher-order functions such as executive functioning—a task that can assess how a person puts together a complex set of information, or a sequence of tasks, that go beyond testing of one domain of cognition such as memory. For example, the clock-drawing test is useful because it combines several facets of cognitive function, including visuospatial function and executive function. The patient is asked to draw a circle representing a clock, place all the numbers, and place the hands to indicate a time (such as 20 minutes past ten o'clock). The performance is somewhat affected by age and education and is not generally sensitive to very mild cases of dementia (von Gunten et al., 2008). But gross errors (such as not including all 12 numbers or a failure to include both hands) are highly indicative of cognitive dysfunction, and the visual record (which should be left in the medical chart) is quite useful in demonstrating the degree of impairment to the treatment team and others.

The EXIT-15 tests executive function and could be used to supplement the MMSE (Royall & Mahurin, 1994). It may be too long to be used routinely, but a clinician may select items from it (many of which are already commonly used in clinical settings by CL psychiatrists) for clinical purposes and become familiar with its properties.

Story problems might be appropriate for some patients, such as, "If I gave you 6 books and you had to separate them on two shelves so that one shelf had twice as many books as the other, how would you divide the 6 books?" (A favorite of my old supervisor, Dr. Ned Cassem.) Usually, it is not just the incorrectness of the answer but the lack of insight into the incorrectness of the given answer, or the grossly implausible nature of the incorrect answer, that is informative. Another brief task that could be used is the Frank Jones story: "I have a friend, Frank Jones, whose feet are so big he has to put his pants on over his head. How does that strike you?" (Bechtold, Horner, Labbate, & Windham, 2001; Cassem & Murray, 1997). The take-home point regarding these brief tests is that a clinician should develop a repertoire for use in an overall cognitive screening examination.

ASSESSING PSYCHIATRIC SYMPTOMS

In terms of assessing psychiatric symptoms that could interfere with decision making, the clinician should review the commonly included psychiatric mental status items such as for hallucinations, potential delusional thoughts, and assessing the degree of organization of the patient's thought processes. One should screen, if appropriate, for major disorders, such as bipolar disorder, major depression, anxiety disorders. Suicidality needs to be assessed, especially in patients with depression.

Assessment of Abilities Relevant to Treatment Consent Capacity

Next the examiner will begin examining more directly the patient's consent-related abilities. Those abilities have been discussed earlier (see chapter 2). Although these abilities are discussed in order here, in reality the competency evaluator does not necessarily follow this order in every case. In fact, although in this chapter the assessment of clinical symptoms is discussed ahead of the assessment of decisional abilities, the evaluator may in fact need to be flexible in actual practice.

Understanding

By this point in the evaluation, the capacity evaluator will have reviewed the patient's medical decision-making situation sufficiently to be able to disclose all of the following elements to the patient:

- The patient's medical condition
- The proposed intervention, whether diagnostic (e.g., a biopsy) or a treatment (e.g., placement of a pacemaker)
- The rationale—typically the hoped-for benefit—of the intervention, as well as the most important risks, and their likelihood
- The alternatives to the proposed intervention (including the option of not doing anything at all) and the associated benefits and risks of each, and their likelihood

The evaluator begins by disclosing (or, more likely, redisclosing) these items to the patient. The evaluator must be familiar enough with the situation-specific items so that a reasonably accurate lay version of the above items can be explained to the patient. This is crucial because it will not always be clear what the patient has been told, and even if the domains have been covered by the treatment team, they may not have been disclosed with appropriately adjusted language for the patient.

UNDERSTANDING VERSUS APPRECIATION

Recall that the standard of understanding involves a meaning of the word that is a bit narrower than the common use of the term "understanding." Of course, the patient may answer the questions in such a way that she correctly applies the facts to his own situation (thus showing appreciation). But the capacity evaluator needs to keep the conceptual points distinct. A lack of appreciation that is based on poor understanding could be remediated by better disclosure or education of the patient; but lack of appreciation despite good understanding may need to be explored from a different angle.

Prefacing the factual comprehension questions with "what have the doctors told you about . . .?" is a good way to isolate the ability to understand from the ability to appreciate. For example, one might follow up an initial question of "Why are you in the hospital?" with "What have the doctors told you so far about what might be wrong?" This allows the patient who may be delusional and who does not agree with what he has been told to at least articulate the facts that have been told to him.

In testing understanding, giving the patient an opportunity to demonstrate that she has processed the information can be very useful: "In your own words, what is the procedure that the doctors are saying you need?"

CONTEXT-SPECIFIC INFORMATION

There may be particularly salient aspects to the situation that need specific attention. For example, if the risk–benefit situation is such that the decision is "preference sensitive" (i.e., a choice without a clear, dominant option that is obviously better than the others), then it is important to make sure that the patient is capable of understanding the essential differentiating aspects of each option. For example, option A may be very invasive with slightly greater risk of death, but also with a greater chance of benefit than option B, which is less invasive but also less beneficial. In such a situation, the evaluator should assess whether the patient is capable of ordering the two options along the risk continuum and also on the benefit continuum.

UNDERSTANDING AND MEMORY

The relationship between memory and understanding sometimes raises concerns. Understanding relies on memory, but it is an unsettled question how long the patient must retain the information in order to be considered competent. Obviously, retention of information is necessary for at least a short term, because it takes some amount of time to make and communicate a stable choice. But beyond this, there is no clearly accepted standard. Some believe that the requirement for retention should not be too extensive. For example, one of the most recent laws on consent capacity (the Mental Capacity Act 2005 of England and Wales that took effect in 2007) states, "The fact that a person is able to retain the information relevant to a decision for a short period only does not prevent him from being regarded as able to make the decision." At minimum, it seems that the patient needs to retain the information long enough to provide a stable situation for implementation of the choice made by the patient.

5
chapter

ENHANCING UNDERSTANDING

Lastly, the evaluator should remember to use techniques necessary to enhance the understanding of the patient. This could include adapting one's language level to accommodate the patient's education level and simplifying the disclosure (Tymchuk et al., 1986), breaking up disclosure elements into manageable amounts (rather than a long, extended disclosure) (Dellasega et al., 1996; Grisso & Appelbaum, 1995), and in general educating the patient with complementary sources of information or repeating key information with correction of errors (Dunn et al., 2001; Wirshing et al., 1998).

Appreciation

The appreciation standard can be assessed as a natural follow-up to the questions asked during the assessment of understanding. For example, after asking, "What have the doctors told you about your condition?" it is natural to follow up with, "Well, what do you think about what the doctors told you? Do you understand what that means for your situation?" Or, following up "What are they saying is the best option for you right now to treat your condition?" with "Do you agree with them?" In general, whereas in the assessment of understanding the focus is on "What do the doctors say...," in the appreciation assessment, the questions will focus on what the patient believes will happen to her specifically. So, for example, the patient might be able to state that the doctors have said that ECT will alleviate the patient's depression but the patient may not believe that it will benefit her.

In some ways, the assessment of the appreciation ability is the most conceptually complicated element in the capacity interview. Figure 5.1 is a flow diagram to help the evaluator think through the elements necessary to meet the appreciation standard.

APPRECIATION REQUIRES INTACT UNDERSTANDING

A patient who is not able to understand the key disclosure elements of informed consent for treatment will not be in a position to demonstrate his ability to appreciate how those facts apply to him. Thus, the assessment of appreciation builds on the assessment of understanding, much in the way that verbal memory testing cannot occur in an aphasic patient or in a patient who has disrupted attention. Of course, from the point of view of judging the person's treatment consent capacity, this may not matter, because the understanding standard is a universally acknowledged requirement for capacity, and a failure in that ability is sufficient to deem someone incompetent, regardless of its implications for the other abilities. However, as we have seen, there is considerable evidence that understanding can be improved, in persons with a variety of conditions. Thus, isolating the source of apparent lack of appreciation as a lack of understanding could be important in ensuring that the evaluator has taken all appropriate steps to maximize the patient's understanding.

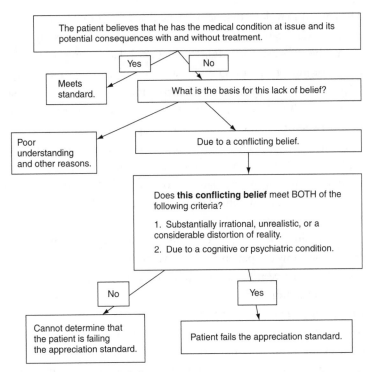

Figure 5.1 Flow Diagram for Assessment of Appreciation Standard

When patients apparently retain their understanding ability, it will be fairly obvious when a careful assessment of the appreciation ability will be necessary because most layperson statements regarding the main disclosure elements for informed consent (i.e., patient's condition, the proposed intervention and its risks and benefits, etc.) usually involve belief statements. For example, when asked, "What are the doctors telling you is going on?" the patient whose understanding is intact will not only discuss what the doctors are saying but also express her opinion or belief as well.

BASIS FOR LACK OF APPRECIATION

One can see from Figure 5.1 that the assessment of the ability to appreciate involves more than just determining whether a person has accurate beliefs. The process ensures that capacity evaluators do not use their personal judgments or disagreements with the patient's beliefs as the basis for determining someone incompetent.

The patient may deny that he has a medical condition in question or deny its implications with or without treatment. This by itself cannot be the basis for judging someone to lack appreciation. The evaluator must further establish that this denial is due to some type of pathology that manifests in a substantially irrational belief that conflicts with it. In essence, the evaluator must judge the connection between the patient's beliefs and cognitive or psychiatric dysfunction. This is an important point because a superficial understanding of the evaluation process may make it seem as though the job of the evaluator is to be an arbiter of the patient's worldview or value system. The focus is rather to find out how the required appreciation is disrupted.

Thus, an important part of evaluating the ability to appreciate is to consider how the patient's cognitive or psychiatric symptoms are related to her responses to probes regarding appreciation. The clinical evaluation and the capacity evaluation cannot be separated. In considering how to best assess the ability to appreciate, it is useful to consider some typical ways in which a patient may fail the standard. Aside from the quite common situation of a lack of understanding underlying the apparent lack of appreciation (discussed above), the evaluator should consider the following types of situations.

First, the patient may be under a delusion caused by one of many psychiatric (schizophrenia, schizoaffective disorder, bipolar disorder, major depressive disorder, delusional disorder, etc.) or other medical conditions (mainly delirium and dementias due to a variety of causes). Thus, a patient may be able to articulate what the team doctors have told him but persist in a delusion that prevents him from accepting that medical opinion (e.g., that the doctors are not really doctors but actually government agents). Unfortunately, a patient who is paranoid about her delusion may hide that belief, and the only surface manifestation may be an enigmatic denial or disagreement. A hidden delusion can place the evaluator in a very difficult situation indeed.

Second, some patients may not have an outright delusion but have a remarkably narrowed "field of vision," as it were, that is a severe distortion of their own values (i.e., premorbid values and beliefs). An example would be a severely depressed person who has an impenetrable belief, a kind of rigid pessimism, that "there are no other options but to accept my death" and who refuses treatment on that basis. This assessment can actually be quite difficult if the patient also has a serious medical condition that is difficult to treat because it may not be clear whether the apparent "acceptance of death" is an understandable adaptation or a nihilism sometimes associated with severe depression (Wenger & Halpern, 1994).

Third, some patients lack insight into their own condition—that is, the failure to realize that one is suffering from the illness or condition in question—as a direct result of their illnesses. This lack of insight can be part of a variety of conditions such as dementia, delirium, psychotic illnesses, brain injury, stroke, seizures, and mania. In such cases, the constellation of symptoms that are part of the syndrome or the condition will help the evaluator see that the lack of belief is a manifestation of an illness, one symptom among many that constitute the condition.

In general, the evaluator needs to carefully and in a nonthreatening manner probe the basis for the patient's underlying belief that is preventing him from accepting the nature of his condition and/or its likely consequence with or without treatment. Some of the more difficult cases in interpretation are discussed in detail in chapter 6.

Choice

By this point, in the testing of the patient's understanding and appreciation abilities, the patient may already have expressed her treatment preference. Indeed, because quite often it is the patient's apparently "irrational" (at least to the treatment team) choice that triggers the capacity consultation, the evaluator may already be aware of the patient's preference. However, this is a good place to revisit the patient's choice, and ask, "Now that we have talked about your condition and the recommended treatment, what do you think you'd like to do?" This naturally leads to an examination of the patient's ability to reason, as the evaluator begins to probe the rationale behind the stated choice.

Reasoning

In thinking about how best to gather data about a patient's reasoning ability, it is worth remembering that no jurisdiction seems to rely *only* on the reasoning standard (Berg et al., 1996). There is a good reason for this: An incapacitated person almost always will have additional impairments in other domains. Thus, the assessment of the reasoning ability plays a slightly different function in the overall capacity assessment. It can aid in the discovery of impairments in other domains, most commonly in the ability to apply the facts of the situation to oneself, that is, appreciation standard. Impairments of the two domains often travel together. A hidden deficit in understanding or appreciation will manifest as an apparent lack of reasoning. Assessment of reasoning, more often than not, serves as a probe.

The evaluator should assess the patient's reasoning ability in two ways. First, it is often quite natural to integrate it into the assessment of one of the other abilities. Careful probing and clarifications of the patient's responses to the understanding or appreciation questions will naturally involve probes into the way the patient processes the information. In this sense, a careful and curious interviewer cannot help but assess for some key aspects of reasoning in the process of exploring the patient's understanding and appreciation abilities. For instance, when a patient exhibits two apparently contradictory beliefs, the evaluator will naturally probe and try to understand how the patient could hold those two beliefs ("You said that you do not want treatment X, which is the only life-saving treatment available, but you also said you do not want to die. Can you tell me then why you are refusing treatment X?"). It is more likely that there is a hidden premise (not shared with the evaluator) that makes it "rational" to the patient, rather than that patient's primary problem being an inability to follow the simple logic of A and not A being incompatible. Thus, the evaluator, in the process of assessing the patient's reasoning, is also assessing for an underlying belief that may be preventing the patient from properly appreciating his situation.

Or, when a patient appears to lack the ability to properly balance or weigh different key considerations and seems obsessively and narrowly focused on one option, it is more likely that an overwhelming emotional factor (extreme fear, for instance) is affecting the processing of the information rather than a primary breakdown in the reasoning ability. Again, probing the patient's underlying rationale is also a probing of the patient's understanding and appreciation abilities as well.

Second, the evaluator will supplement these probes with more direct questions about how the patient is going from her premises to her conclusion (choice). The evaluator will seek an explanation for the choice that the patient has expressed, as well as an explanation regarding rejection of other options. The evaluator can ask, "Can you tell me why you would rather have that procedure done?" or "Why would you rather not have the alternative procedure done?" "In your opinion, why is that choice better than the other?" "Can you talk about how these different treatment options might affect your everyday life?" "In your mind, what are the most important reasons for choosing X?" In evaluating patients' answers to these questions, it is important to not set the threshold too high for what is an acceptable answer. The purpose is not to elicit a comprehensive recitation of the rationales and line of reasoning leading to the choice, but rather to detect obvious deficiencies in the process. As noted, generally it is much more likely that the apparent breakdown in reasoning is a manifestation of another hidden issue in understanding or appreciation, rather than a primary breakdown in reasoning. When the latter does occur, it usually signals significant brain dysfunction accompanied by significant impairment in other domains that is difficult to miss.

Structured Instruments for Clinical Use: Advantages and Limitations

In chapter 3, as part of a review of the empirical literature on consent capacity, we listed the many interview instruments that have been used to evaluate the consent capacity of patients in a variety of research studies. (See Table 3.1.) How might these instruments be of use to the capacity evaluator? Should one use an instrument during actual capacity evaluations? Although the question seems a natural one, it raises a host of issues. In this section, we first discuss the issues involved when one attempts to use an instrument for assessing capacity in the clinical setting. We then discuss and compare in some detail two instruments that are perhaps the most widely cited in the literature.

Limitations and Advantages of Structured Instruments

LIMITS

Although the use of a structured instrument for assessing capacity seems straightforward, there are some preliminary issues to deal with. First, a capacity instrument for use in most clinical settings is not a standardized instrument. The clinical evaluator assesses patients with various causes of impairment, facing a variety of medical decisions of varying benefits and risks. Whereas a cognitive mental status screen (in which the same items are administered to all subjects) can be standardized, one can standardize a capacity instrument only for specially narrow contexts (for persons with same illness, facing similar decisions). For research purposes, one can of course use hypothetical scenarios, but the normative justification of such a procedure for the clinical context seems doubtful, given the modern emphasis on decision-specific assessments of capacity. That is, testing a surgical patient using a hypothetical dementia scenario might be very informative about that patient's potential for making capable decisions, but then one would not be testing the patient's capacity to make the decision at hand as it applies to him. Usually, the instrument itself needs to be adapted to sufficiently reflect the patient's specific decision-making situation.

Second, although a capacity instrument can contribute valuable information to the evaluation process, it is not possible to impose a decision-making rule solely based on the outcome of the structured evaluation. Instruments at best measure degrees and types of impairment. Additional clinical judgment is necessary to arrive at a categorical judgment. This often overlooked issue is discussed in much more detail in chapter 6.

Third, the instrument has to be user friendly. For example, the original MacArthur research instruments were designed specifically for research purposes and are impractical for the clinical context due to their length and procedural complexity (Grisso et al., 1995).

Fourth, the instrument has to validly conceptualize and implement the legal standards for treatment consent capacity. The instrument needs to adequately and explicitly cover the relevant legal standards such that the evaluator can document which legally relevant ability was measured and what the outcome was. In this regard, some instruments measure only the ability to understand, or do not measure all four abilities—perhaps the most common deficiency of several published instruments (Dunn et al., 2006). An extreme case is the Hopkins Competency Assessment Test, which is called a "competency assessment test," but which essentially measures the patient's knowledge about the concept of informed consent rather than a patient's ability to make a medical decision (Kim et al., 2002b; Moye, 2003).

Given the above issues, it should be clear that a capacity instrument in the clinical setting is at best an interview aid for assessing the abilities relevant to treatment consent capacity.

ADVANTAGES

Using an established instrument—an instrument that has been well conceptualized and operationalized in relation to the accepted legal standards—does have significant advantages. It forces the capacity evaluator to be comprehensive, to use questions and probes that are conceptually on target and have been validated, and allows the capacity evaluator to document the interview in systematic and domain-specific ways. Further, if the instrument has been used in a variety of research studies, the body of evidence gathered using that instrument lends further support for using that instrument.

In certain special contexts—especially when conditions allow the structured interview to function more as a standardized interview, as in certain research consent contexts—the role of the instrument may be even more important and useful. This is discussed further in chapter 8.

Capacity Instruments: Two Examples

Two instruments are worth noting in some detail—the Capacity to Consent to Treatment Instrument (CCTI; Marson et al., 1995b)

5
chapter

and MacCAT-T (Grisso & Appelbaum, 1998). Arguably, the research literature on CCTI and MacCAT-T are the most extensive among all the available capacity instruments. It will be useful for the capacity evaluator to have some in-depth knowledge of these instruments, both in the interpretation of the literature they have generated and in potential adaptation of these instruments for clinical use. Further, these instruments are different from each other in interesting ways, illustrating the subtle yet substantial differences in constructs, in implementation, and in interpretation of the abilities relevant to consent capacity.

CAPACITY TO CONSENT TO TREATMENT INSTRUMENT (CCTI)

The CCTI has primarily been used for research purposes, having been developed by Marson and colleagues as a "prototype" instrument in the mid-1990s and used for all of their subsequent work with only minor changes (Marson et al., 1995b; Marson et al., 2005). There is no a priori reason why it cannot be used for patients with a variety of conditions, but its primary use has been with persons with cognitive impairment (mostly AD), and its relatively disproportionate emphasis on assessing the ability to understand probably reflects this origin (Marson et al., 1995b). Besides being used in AD, it has been used in minimal cognitive impairment and early dementia states (Okonkwo et al., 2007), Parkinson's disease with cognitive impairment (Dymek et al., 2001), and TBI (Marson et al., 2005).

As the title suggests, the CCTI focuses on treatment consent capacity. Like all capacity instruments, it does not generate a universally applicable cutoff score. The instrument assesses the abilities relevant to capacity by testing the subject using two clinical vignettes presenting two hypothetical medical problems (cardiovascular disease and brain tumor), which contain the necessary disclosure elements of informed consent. Each vignette is written in fifth to sixth grade reading level. At least for the published studies, these vignettes are read in their entirety to the subjects as they follow along, before questions are asked. The decisional abilities are assessed by follow-up questions that explore five legal domains, whose features reveal some subtle but important construct issues in the CCTI.

Evidencing a choice is assessed by a single item asking which treatment option the patient would choose. *Ability to make a reasonable choice* uses a single item. This item assesses whether the *content* of the choice is reasonable. The authors correctly note that this item is for research purposes only, as it is a criterion long discarded for assessing capacity, as we have discussed in chapter 2. *Ability to appreciate* is described as "the emotional and cognitive consequences of a treatment choice." This is a somewhat confusing description of "appreciation" for the following reasons. One potential confusion is that of labeling. The authors cite the Roth et al. (1977) article as the source of this standard. However, that article does not use the term "appreciation standard." Rather, it discusses a "rational reasons" standard, using a delusional patient as a prototypical example (thus, Roth et al.'s "rational reasons" standard is indeed a precursor to the appreciation standard). Unfortunately, the CCTI uses the same term, "rational reasons," to refer to a "reasoning" standard. A second potential source of confusion for the evaluator who attempts to use the CCTI's appreciation standard is more substantive. It is conceptually somewhat different from the "appreciation" standard we have been discussing in this book. CCTI's appreciation standard tends to focus more on the acknowledgment of "consequences" rather than on the insight that the patient needs to show in applying the facts to her own situation. This conceptual point is clearly evident in the fact that the CCTI relies on hypothetical vignettes—and by necessity uses diagnoses that the patients may not have. Under the four abilities model discussed in this book, a key component of the appreciation standard is the insight into the fact that one is suffering from the illness in question. Thus, when using normal controls (people for whom having an insight into having the disease in question is not applicable) to test capacity instruments, other researchers have not tested the appreciation ability in that group (Grisso et al., 1997; Palmer et al., 2004). For these reasons, the capacity evaluator who uses the CCTI should be aware that what is being measured is something conceptually related yet different from the appreciation standard that is being used in this book.

5
chapter

Ability to provide "rational reasons" for the choice essentially asks the patient to generate reasons for their choices. It is confusing that the authors used this term from the Roth et al. (1977) paper, which, as we have noted, the original authors used to denote something akin to the appreciation standard and which Marson et al. cite in support of their appreciation standard. As used in the CCTI, the rational reasons standard is designed to measure the reasoning ability discussed by Appelbaum and Grisso (1988), and should not be confused with the Roth et al. use of the term. *Ability to understand the treatment situation and choices* is assessed by nine items, by far the longest section of the interview.

A manual can be obtained from the first author of the instrument (Marson et al., 1995b), as it is not published. The interview is said to take about 20–25 min. The authors report that their scoring criteria are highly reliable (correlation of .83 for interval scales, i.e., the ability to appreciate, reason, and understand; 96% agreement for single-item measures). The scores for each ability are summed across the results of the two vignettes, and the total scores are used as a measure of the person's abilities. As noted already, there are no a priori cutoff threshold scores.

The evaluator has two choices in using the CCTI. It could be implemented with the two prewritten vignettes that have been used in the authors' published studies. The advantage of this is that the evaluator will be able to compare the scores from published studies with one's own practice, and there is no need to construct a new set of disclosure elements. But then the assessment will in fact not be decision specific. This raises the question of whether the CCTI used in that way can be considered a capacity assessment tool that conforms to the modern understanding of treatment consent capacity as a decision- and situation-specific concept, as discussed in chapter 2.

Alternatively, the evaluator can construct a vignette that is decision specific, or simply disclose the decision-specific elements as one would do in real-time evaluations, and then use the questions, suitably adapted, in the CCTI for assessment of the abilities. The advantage of this approach is that the questions are well grounded in the research and ethico-legal literature (but of course understanding that the "appreciation" standard may be somewhat different), providing good content validity for the relevant capacity domains. In neither approach, however, is there a cutoff score that can be used across contexts. The evaluator must use the results of the interview to arrive at the dichotomous judgment. Moye (2003) provides an excellent and thorough review of the CCTI.

MACARTHUR COMPETENCE ASSESSMENT TOOL—TREATMENT (MACCAT-T)

The MacArthur instruments are the best-known instruments for assessing decision-making capacity in both treatment and research consent settings. The authors of these instruments first used several research instruments in the original MacArthur Treatment Competence Study published in 1995 (Appelbaum & Grisso, 1995; Grisso & Appelbaum, 1995; Grisso et al., 1995). There were separate instruments for the assessment of understanding (Understanding Treatment Disclosures [UTD]), appreciation (Perception of Disorder [POD]), and reasoning (Thinking Rationally About Treatment [TRAT], which included an item for evidencing a choice). On the basis of this large study, the authors developed a shorter, more user-friendly MacCAT-T, which only takes about 20 min to complete and contains sections for all four domains relevant to capacity (Grisso et al., 1997). Studies involving persons with dementia, medical illnesses (cardiac illness, diabetes), schizophrenia, and depression have been conducted using the MacCAT-T (Grisso et al., 1997; Palmer et al., 2004).

The instrument's disclosure elements are specific to the patient's decision-making situation; these must be adapted by the evaluator. Unlike the CCTI, the disclosure is not given in its entirety but is given in parts to maximize understanding by the subject. Thus, facts relevant to the understanding of the disorder, of the nature of the proposed treatment, and of the risks and benefits are evaluated separately. One useful feature of the scoring scheme for the understanding section is that the section total score is adjusted for the number of disclosure questions asked (which in theory could vary from one decision situation to next) so that it can be used to compare the scores with those from published studies.

5
chapter

The appreciation section tests two items—whether the patient is able to apply the facts of the disorder and of the treatment options to his situation. The reasoning section examines consequential reasoning, comparative reasoning, generation of consequences to everyday life, and logical consistency.

Unlike the CCTI and many other instruments found in the literature, the MacCAT-T is explicitly designed to be used day to day in the clinic. The content validity of the MacCAT-T is high as it is based on extensive and rigorous ethico-legal review. It can be administered and scored with a high degree of reliability (Grisso & Appelbaum, 1998, p. 191; Grisso et al., 1997). The manual and a training video for the instrument is available (http://www.prpress. com/books/mact-setfr.html). Because it can be tailored to each treatment consent situation, the MacCAT-T provides a decision-specific guide to assessing capacity. The MacCAT-T, like the CCTI and all other capacity instruments intended to be used across a variety of illnesses and situations, does not provide a method for going from the numerical scores generated by the interview to a judgment about capacity. Judgment must be supplied by the evaluator.

Interpretation $\bigg|$ 6

The main purpose behind a capacity evaluation is to correctly determine whether the patient should retain the authority to make a medical treatment decision. Assuming that the capacity evaluator has assessed a patient's specific decision-making abilities relevant to treatment consent, as outlined in earlier chapters, a major question still remains: How impaired must a patient be to be considered too impaired to provide valid informed consent? On the surface, it appears as though we could simply arrive at a consensus regarding a reasonable threshold to apply, using the results of a patient's performance on, for instance, one of the many competency assessment instruments discussed.

Unfortunately, the concept of consent capacity delineated in chapters 1 and 2 implies that the task of going from assessing the relevant decisional abilities to determining the categorical capacity status of a patient is more complicated. This is because the accepted framework for capacity assessments does not rely on an absolute level of ability that will always designate competence or incompetence. Rather, the modern concept of capacity implies that a categorical judgment of capacity status has several aspects, as reflected in the following question: Does this patient's current level of functioning as exhibited by his (a) *functionally relevant decisional abilities*, (b) *in the current decision-making context*, (c) meet a *minimum threshold to be deemed competent* to make his own medical decision at issue?

This chapter discusses each of the components in this judgment. The first component is the performance exhibited by the patient on the relevant abilities for treatment consent. Some of the lessons learned from decisional capacity research will be used to illustrate the challenges of translating dimensional data into categorical judgments.

The second component consists of the important contextual considerations—the most important of these being the risk–benefit profile of the consent context. This chapter reviews the approaches advocated by some of the leading scholars on how to frame the risk–benefit considerations that should be incorporated into a capacity judgment.

The third component is the act by the evaluator of bringing together the patient's performance factors and the risk–benefit context, using a standard that presumably reflects our society's values—as reflected in law—regarding how such a capacity judgment should be made. Some of the challenges of making judgments about patients' competence are illustrated using the results of a survey of consultation psychiatrists.

Despite these guidelines, ultimately a determination of treatment consent capacity requires a judgment that is often quite challenging. This chapter will discuss several examples of particularly difficult types of cases, as a way of demonstrating how even in such cases, following a systematic framework can lead to reasonable judgments. The chapter will close with a brief discussion on documentation.

Relevant Abilities

Functionally Relevant Abilities

The four abilities model has been discussed in chapter 2, which focused on conceptual and legal foundations, and in chapter 5, which applied these concepts to the patient interview. Although there are exceptions, state statutes, court cases, and hospital policies often refer to some or all of the four standards that are discussed in this book: evidencing a choice, understanding, appreciation, and reasoning. Recall that there is an overlap in meaning between the various standards articulated in statutes or policies and the four abilities model, such that one can often interpret the local standards in terms of one or more of the four abilities. The capacity evaluator needs to understand her own jurisdiction's specific requirements and their relationship to the four abilities model, as some jurisdictions may in fact have important precedents to the contrary, such as explicitly rejecting the appreciation standard (Grisso & Appelbaum, 1998).

Can the Relevant Abilities Be Validly and Reliably Measured?

Reliability refers to reproducibility of an outcome between interviewers, between scorers (based on the same interview), or across time (test–retest). In all these dimensions, instruments that measure specific abilities relevant to capacity have been shown to be reasonably reliable. Further, these abilities can be validly measured. There are various types of validity, all of which address whether the instrument or the interview measures what it purports to measure. Indeed, the field of capacity research has made considerable strides in the development of methods to measure the individual abilities quite reliably and validly (Dunn et al., 2006; Kim et al., 2002b; Moye, 2003). An interviewer who systematically and carefully follows the guidance of some of the more tested instruments, such as the MacArthur instruments, should be able to reliably and validly measure these abilities.

Translating Measurements of Abilities into Dichotomous Judgments

Although the relevant abilities can be reliably and validly measured, something more than measurement is required to translate the data into a categorical judgment. We can use the following situation to illustrate this point. Assume that a capacity evaluator has chosen to use a particular capacity interview instrument (e.g., MacCAT-T) and has reliably and validly measured the understanding ability of a patient, arriving at a score that indicates a certain level of ability. (Although this example assumes the use of an instrument to demonstrate this point, the conceptual issues are similar for an evaluator who uses a more informal, clinical approach.) How does one know whether or not this score, in the specified context, falls above or below a capacity threshold? Here it may be instructive to examine the variety of approaches taken by researchers who face the same problem in their research studies.

A PRIORI THRESHOLD

Some researchers have simply set an a priori threshold (Wirshing et al., 1998). Such an approach reflects the intuitions of those setting the threshold but may not reflect a broader societal perspective. Translated into the clinical context for a clinician using a capacity instrument, it means that he could designate a priori a level of performance as a cutoff threshold but it will be unclear how this threshold reflects societal values.

STATISTICAL THRESHOLD

Other researchers have used a psychometric approach, using a statistical cutoff—for example, persons scoring 2 SD below the mean score of a control group could be classified as incapable on the standard in question (Grisso et al., 1997; Marson et al., 1995b; Schmand et al., 1999). The advantage of this approach is that it provides an excellent sense of the relative performance of the patient, either in relation to the patient group as a whole or in comparison to a relevant control group. The disadvantage is that there is no intrinsic ethical meaning to the statistical cutoff. For one thing, it takes no account of society's values in balancing autonomy and welfare in considering the decisional authority of an impaired patient because it does not take into account the risk–benefit context of the decision at issue.

EXPERTS' JUDGMENT THRESHOLD

Another approach has been to establish a cutoff threshold by using professionals with expertise in capacity assessments and asking them to provide judgments that can be used as a provisional reference standard (Etchells et al., 1999; Fazel et al., 1999; Kim et al., 2001; Kim et al., 2007). This approach has some advantages. First, to the extent that such experts incorporate the risk–benefit context into their judgments, the results incorporate a key ethical dimension lacking in purely psychometric approaches. Second, in fact our society currently relies on expert judgments for capacity judgments so this approach has prima facie support. Third, it provides an independent validation of the capacity interview. Finally, for stereotyped situations (such as research consent), it may be possible to validate thresholds on scores resulting from screening instruments

using this method, providing benchmark scores for use in similar future contexts (see chapter 8). There are also drawbacks to this expert judgment-based validation, including the obvious question of how the experts in the study are supposed to make their own judgments. Indeed, there are mixed results regarding the variability of clinician judgments, as we saw. However, as discussed in chapter 3, most well-designed studies (e.g., using several experts' views rather than just one) using expert judgment standards have proven reliable. For a clinician using an instrument for assessing the decisional abilities for the treatment context, there is a relatively small evidence base regarding how experienced clinicians would use the instrument to establish cutoff scores. But future research may address this shortcoming.

The main point is that although it is not difficult to accurately assess the individual abilities relevant to capacity—indeed, the evidence is that we can do so reliably and validly—the task of translating such measurements into categorical determinations of capacity is not straightforward, especially for a clinician faced with a patient whose situation may be different from the situation depicted in the published research studies. At the end of the day, there will not be any algorithms but there are several important considerations to keep in mind.

6
chapter

The Context: Risks and Potential Benefits of Treatment Options

Consent capacity is a relational concept that encompasses both the abilities of the patient and the decision's contextual factors (Buchanan & Brock, 1989). Among the contextual factors, two issues are most frequently mentioned: the complexity of the decision-making situation and the risk–benefit context.

Performance Demand Context

As Grisso (2003) has described, judgments about competence always require weighing the degree of ability of the patient against the "degree of performance demand" of the situation. For example, in the forensic context, a defendant with a certain level of functional abilities may be competent to stand trial if it is simple and brief but the same level of functioning may not be sufficient for a complex and lengthy trial (Grisso, 2003).

This need to take into account the complexity of the decision is mentioned by other writers; for example, the rationale for a certain procedure might be rather complex, or the procedure itself may involve difficult concepts (Buchanan & Brock, 1989, p. 55).

How should the complexity of the decision-making situation be taken into account? It is *not* through an alteration of the capacity threshold—the idea that if the demand of the decision task is high, then the threshold for capacity should be set high, so that the person exhibits a higher level of abilities in order to be deemed competent. This is because the performance demand principle is simply an extension of the idea that a person's capacity should be assessed in terms of the task or decision at issue rather than be based on a global label of "unsoundness of mind" or assuming that simply because she lacks the capacity for one task that she lacks the capacity for another task or decision. In fact, by focusing on the actual task in the assessment of the abilities relevant to competence (i.e., the patient's understanding and appreciation of the situation, and his reasoning and choice tailored to the actual decision at hand), this "performance demand" issue is already factored into the overall evaluation (Grisso & Appelbaum, 1998, p. 136). There is no need to "adjust" the threshold for capacity for the performance demand required, because if the assessment of the abilities is done correctly (i.e., assessment of each ability has been properly contextualized to the task at hand), it will already have been factored into the overall assessment. This is different from what must be done in incorporating another contextual factor, namely, the risk–benefit profile of the treatment options.

Risk–Benefit Context

If a patient has expressed a treatment preference, then that option's particular risks and potential benefits must be assessed and used in setting the threshold for capacity. This means that the patient may be considered competent to make one decision while not competent to make the opposite or different choice. On its face, this may seem paternalistic, and some philosophers have criticized this type of risk-sensitive standard as providing too high a hurdle when the risk is high and too low a standard when the risks are minimal (Wicclair, 1991). It may seem to some that we are returning to the paternalistic standard of "you are competent if you agree with the doctor, but incompetent if you disagree." As was discussed in chapter 2, this is not the case.

As long as considerations of welfare—risks and potential benefits—are included in the overall interpretive framework, the possibility of a patient being capable of choosing one option and yet not being capable of choosing the opposite option exists. Although this apparent paradox is not always explicitly stated, it is implied by the wide agreement in law and ethics that a capacity evaluation must incorporate welfare considerations (National Bioethics Advisory Commission, 1998; President's Commission, 1982).

There is no established, specific method of weighing the risks and burdens against the potential benefits of a proposed treatment that must be incorporated into a capacity assessment. Different writers have used different illustrative schemes to organize and evaluate risk–benefit categories of potential decision-making situations (Buchanan & Brock, 1989, p. 53; Grisso et al., 1998, pp. 138–139). Two such approaches are discussed here.

Buchanan and Brock in their landmark book *Deciding for Others* discuss how much ability is required for different types of circumstances, using three examples:

- a patient who consents to lumbar puncture for presumed meningitis,
- a patient who chooses lumpectomy for breast cancer, and
- a patient who refuses surgery for simple appendectomy.

The Buchanan and Brock approach emphasizes comparing the risk–benefit balance of the patient's choice with that of other available

6
chapter

alternatives—that is, their approach focuses on *relative* benefits and risks of the treatment options. An important justification for using a "low/minimal" level of decision-making abilities threshold for capacity for the first case (patient with suspected meningitis who consents to a procedure) is that in comparison with other alternatives, the "net balance" of risk/benefits is "substantially better." On the other hand, the patient who refuses potentially life-saving surgery is choosing an option, in comparison to other options, that has substantially worse net balance of risks and benefits, and thus requires "high/maximal" level of competence. The middle case is said to require "moderate/ median" level of competence because the patient's choice is assumed to have a net balance of risks/benefits that is "roughly comparable to that of other alternatives." Of course, the use of this final example confounds the "relative" net balance of risks/benefits issue with the absolute level of risks/benefits. The reason why a "moderate/ median" level of competence is required in the example is not simply that the patient's choice carries a risk–benefit profile comparable to that of other options, but also that the medical situation is rather serious, involving cancer, surgery, and matters of survival. If the medical decision were about a low-risk outcome where the various alternatives carried similar net balance of risks and benefits, the correct threshold for competence may well be quite low.

The approach taken by other writers, such as Grisso and Appelbaum (1998), build on the Buchanan and Brock approach but place more emphasis on nonrelative aspects of risks and benefits (while agreeing with most of the elements of the Buchanan–Brock position). These authors use the metaphor of a "competence balance scale," with reasons in favor of welfare on one end and reasons in favor of autonomy on the other. This mental picture of a balance raises the question of where the fulcrum should be placed. The authors believe that given our society's strong emphasis on autonomy, the fulcrum should be placed in favor of giving more weight to autonomy considerations so that, before any reasons are added to either end of the scale, the balance begins in favor of autonomy (p. 131).

By use of the fulcrum analogy, the relative and absolute risk–benefit considerations can be combined. Thus, Grisso and Appelbaum use as an illustration a scheme with four categories of risk–benefit balance:

high probable gain–low risk, moderate probable gain–moderate risk, high probable gain–high risk, and low probable gain–low risk. Note that these are "absolute" (not relative to other options) risks and benefits of the treatment option chosen by the patient. They then accommodate the issue of relative net balance of risk–benefit by moving the fulcrum; for example, if the patient's choice is an option that is relatively less favorable in terms of risks and benefits than the other options the patient could have chosen, the fulcrum is moved in favor of giving greater weight to welfare considerations (p. 140).

In summary, when incorporating risk–benefit factors, the evaluator should ask the following questions, taking into account both the probability and magnitude of each:

- Are the reasonably anticipated risks and burdens high or low (or, high, moderate, or low)?
- Are the reasonably anticipated benefits high or low (or, high, moderate, or low)?
- Finally, how do the risks and benefits of the patient's chosen course compare with the risk–benefit profile of other alternatives (including no treatment at all)?

If the "competence balance scale" makes intuitive sense to an evaluator, she may further reflect on where to place the fulcrum. Admittedly, these are rather broadly guiding notions. There are no empirical studies that show that medical personnel and capacity evaluators converge on their risk–benefit assessments. However, it is reasonable to assume that by systematically asking these questions and making these risk–benefit assessments explicit, and when needed, communicating with the treatment team to clarify her own understanding of the risk–benefit situation, the capacity evaluator should be able to reach a medically sound assessment of the risks and benefits.

6
chapter

Categorical Judgments—Some Considerations

After the capacity evaluator has assessed the functional decisional abilities of the patient and has arrived at a medically sound assessment of the risk–benefit situation, what further guidance is available in rendering the final categorical judgment? Unfortunately, beyond these fairly broad frameworks, there are no specific weights or algorithms that can be applied to particular cases that eliminate the element of judgment. The most that can be said is that *the judgment should reflect societal values.* The most concrete manifestation of this is when a legally appointed judge determines whether a person is competent. Thus, capacity evaluators are encouraged to make their judgments approximate what a court would decide (Grisso & Appelbaum, 1998). It is important to remember that this is an admonition to behave according to an ideal, rather than an assertion about the universal wisdom of the courts because courts can make mistakes too (Gutheil & Bursztajn, 1986).

Although there are no algorithms for arriving at categorical capacity determinations, there are some considerations that may prove helpful. A variety of such issues are discussed next.

Variability in Judgment

Capacity judgments are judgments—implying a process that cannot be reduced to a simple mechanism—and a certain amount of variability in judgment among equally qualified judges is inevitable. Further, capacity judgments are irreducibly *moral* judgments (Moye, 2003) and this may add to the potential for variability as well. Chapter 3 reviews what is known about the characteristics and behaviors of capacity evaluators. We discuss here some findings from a survey we conducted, which sheds some light on how some of the variability might be reduced.

We conducted an experimental video study in which 99 consultation psychiatrists were randomized to view one of two capacity interviews (one was a low-risk and the other a high-risk scenario, both for research participation) (Kim et al., 2006). We hired a professional actor to act out the scene; the scripts were based on actual interviews, however, so that the performance level was identical in both videos but the contextual factor of risks and benefits was different. Although the consent capacity examined was for research consent, the issue of contextual factors applies generally. Because the study's goal was to assess the impact of risk on capacity thresholds used by clinicians, we intentionally selected a case in which, based on our past experience, the subject scored in the "gray area" range for the various consent-related abilities.

The results showed that for the low-risk scenario interview, 60% of the psychiatrists thought the person portrayed was probably or definitely competent; for the high-risk interview, 30% of the psychiatrists thought the person was probably or definitely competent. On the surface, therefore, the results support the view that these psychiatrists used a risk-sensitive standard of capacity threshold. By examining their responses to a variety of additional survey questions, including ones about risks and benefits, we were able to confirm that the differences among judgments are mediated by the capacity evaluators' perception of risks (Kim et al., 2006).

Although the results of our study confirmed that risk–benefit contextual factors have a definite impact on the psychiatrists' judgments, it is instructive that for both high- and low-risk scenarios, there was a sizable minority who disagreed with the majority judgment (40 and 30%, respectively, for low and high risk scenarios). Aside from risk perception, we could not ascertain any reliable predictors of the capacity judgments of these psychiatrists, such as gender, years in practice, experience in capacity evaluations, among others.

Thus, although most consultation psychiatrists use the risk-sensitive threshold for capacity determinations, there are considerable variations in judgment among evaluators, especially for patients exhibiting partial impairments, that is, for cases in the "gray zone." Note that the above experiment does not talk about sources of variation within each individual capacity evaluator, because only one case was reviewed. But our anecdotal impression, based on working with psychiatrists who have reviewed many cases for our other research studies, is that although evaluators may have different thresholds, each individual evaluator tends to be fairly consistent within his own set of judgments. That is to say, judges may be fairly good at judging the relative performance of different patients, even if they use different thresholds.

One takeaway message from the above is that if a "correct" threshold can be communicated to and adopted by capacity evaluators, then fairly reliable judgments across evaluators should be

6
chapter

possible. In difficult "gray area" cases, it is therefore advisable to discuss one's impressions with another colleague, as a way of challenging one's own threshold standard. The more the number of independent opinions, the more likely will the capacity judgment that incorporates those opinions reflect societal values (Kim, 2006).

Not All Items in a Capacity Interview Are of Equal Importance

Most research studies using structured instruments for assessing the abilities relevant to capacity tend to treat each item in the instrument equally. No item is weighted more heavily than another. But in clinical practice, sometimes there are components in the interview that should be treated with more weight than others. For example, the proposed intervention may involve a small but real risk of serious harm. Suppose that this potential for harm constitutes the main risk of the proposed treatment. A clear failure to understand or appreciate that particular risk, or a failure to use the fact in the overall reasoning process in making the decision, would count as a particularly serious lapse, compared to a failure to understand (or appreciate or reason about) another detail, especially if the patient is accepting that treatment. Conversely, from an evaluator's perspective, it may be more important to ensure that a patient truly understands the potential benefits of a treatment that she is refusing (Grisso & Appelbaum, 1998). Thus, although for discussion purposes we divide the interview phase and the interpretation phase of the capacity evaluation, in fact an experienced consultant should tailor his interview to prioritize the most important elements. Obviously, more time and effort should be spent on those elements in the interview that ought to weigh more.

Ethical Issues in Capacity Determinations: Avoiding Bias

To say that a person is not competent to provide her own informed consent means she no longer has the authority to make her own decision; she needs someone else to make that decision for her. In a society that values autonomy—as reflected in our informed consent laws—this is a profound judgment. The fact that the majority of such judgments are made (and acted upon) in the general medical context without going to court is a sobering reminder of the power and responsibility that is assigned to health care providers in our society.

Given this important responsibility, the capacity evaluator needs to avoid extremes of view regarding the relationship between autonomy and welfare. Do capacity evaluators vary in their weighting of autonomy in relation to welfare? In the above study of consultation psychiatrists, because we could find no factor that correlated significantly with the psychiatrists' judgments, we sent a follow-up letter asking them to describe their attitude toward favoring autonomy versus welfare in capacity judgments. We asked which error in capacity determination was the worse mistake in their opinion: finding an incapable patient capable or finding a capable patient incapable. Note that one could reasonably interpret this question as a test of whether psychiatrists place (or at least say that they place) the fulcrum in favor of autonomy or not. At least in our self-selected sample (i.e., volunteers of our experiment) of psychiatrists, the results were quite surprising.

First, on average, the psychiatrists felt that finding an incapable person capable was the worse mistake (score of 5.8 on a 0–10 scale, where 0 means finding a capable person incapable is the worse mistake and 10 means finding an incapable person capable is the worse mistake). Second, this effect was very modest (because a score of 5.0 would have been "neutral") and there was tremendous variability among the psychiatrists: 29% gave an answer of 0–3 (favoring autonomy), 21% gave an answer of 4–6, and 50% gave an answer of 7–10 (favoring welfare). The slight favoring of welfare considerations over autonomy consideration was confirmed by their answer to another question we asked: "Do you think medical ethics nowadays places not enough or too much emphasis on patient autonomy?" On a 1 (not enough) to 7 (too much) scale, the mean was 4.6 (*SD* 1.2) or just slightly in favor of "too much" autonomy response.

The more important question is whether these psychiatrists' views on the relative importance of autonomy and welfare have any impact on their judgments of capacity. We found no correlation

6
chapter

($r = .03$) between their answers regarding autonomy and welfare and their impressions (given on a 10-point scale) of the capacity status of the subject portrayed in the videos, regardless of the risk level of the scenario. This finding has to be interpreted cautiously as it is based on one judgment among many judges, rather than multiple judgments by each clinician. Also, our study was based on the case of a subject whose performance was in the "gray zone." Perhaps the uncertainty created by such patients overwhelms the impact of one's philosophical leanings—perhaps capacity determinations are very fact sensitive.

Nevertheless, in clinical experience one does occasionally encounter professionals whose perspectives are marked by a strong allegiance to either protection or autonomy. We in fact saw above that 79% of our respondents gave scores of 0–3 or 7–10, indicating a willingness to state somewhat extreme positions. It is possible that these philosophical leanings could bias capacity judgments in some cases, in the long run. Thus it may be worth remembering why it is important to balance the two values of welfare and autonomy in capacity determinations.

Balancing the considerations of autonomy and welfare is one of the key tasks for the evaluator. Overemphasizing autonomy can have its pitfalls. Sometimes modern bioethics tends to make a fetish out of autonomy, where it is assumed that autonomy trumps all other values (Schneider, 1998). But attribution of autonomy depends on the intact consent capacity of the patient. It is well established in modern ethics and law that a competent patient can refuse any and all treatment, even if it would lead to certain death, as would be the case when a life-sustaining treatment is refused. At the end of the day, if the patient is competent, autonomy considerations do seem to trump all welfare considerations.

But what if the patient's competence is in question? In such a situation, one cannot fall back on the priority of autonomy, because the very issue of autonomy is in question. Of course, given our society's high regard for autonomy, even in a capacity evaluation a certain amount of special importance must be attributed to autonomy, as some have noted (Grisso & Appelbaum, 1998). But the point here is that when determining a patient's competence, there is more than autonomy to consider. This is why the contextual factors relating to the risks and potential benefits of the various treatment options are legitimate considerations in a capacity determination.

On the other hand, an overemphasis on a patient's welfare presents its own pitfalls. The history of medicine has steadily moved away from the "doctor knows best" model of patient–doctor relationship. The question of "whose values and preferences?" plays a role in determining what constitutes risks and benefits for the patient. It is not hard to see that if physicians and other health care providers use their own judgments of burdens and benefits, then there is a risk of old-fashioned paternalism.

Of course, there is a modern twist to the problem of paternalism that bears mentioning. It used to be that paternalism was almost synonymous with overtreatment. It was commonly assumed that physicians were interested in keeping patients alive at all costs, as exemplified in landmark legal cases in which the courts had to clarify the autonomy interests of the patient. Indeed, it is a backlash against this type of paternalism that has cemented the modern autonomy-based bioethics. But in modern general hospitals, patients more often than not die after withdrawal or withholding of life-sustaining interventions (Prendergast, Claessens, & Luce, 1998; Sprung et al., 2003). Often, the treatment team realizes far ahead of the family and the patient that the end is near. Indeed, this occurs often enough that one of the "selling points" of clinical ethics consultation is in making more timely decisions to forgo such interventions (Schneiderman, Jecker, & Jonsen, 2003). Thus, in modern hospitals, the pressure on the patients' families is in general not to agree to more treatment, but rather the reverse, and often the pressure applied can be inappropriate (Luce & White, 2007). When such patients are able to communicate but are suspected of being incompetent, the capacity evaluator may well become involved in the sometimes complex dynamics of end-of-life surrogate decision making in the modern intensive care unit (see chapter 7).

Special Situations

Determination of competence is a challenging task even when the patient is cooperative and all relevant information is accessible. There are situations, however, when the capacity evaluator must make inferences and judgments under less than ideal conditions. Examples of such situations are discussed in this section. These situations hardly exhaust the possibilities, but they illustrate a general approach for handling such situations that is congruent with the overall framework of this book. Also discussed here are some examples often raised by trainees regarding the interpretation of the appreciation standard.

When the Patient Is Uncooperative

When a patient whose decision-making capacity may be compromised refuses to be interviewed by the capacity evaluator, the evaluator is forced to make a decision with less than ideal information—an unenviable position. How can the evaluator conduct a professionally competent assessment if the patient does not cooperate? This is an unusual but not a rare occurrence (Grisso & Appelbaum, 1998; Hurst, 2004; Wenger & Halpern, 1994; Youngner, 1998). What should an evaluator do? Although this topic may seem to belong in a chapter on data collection, the special challenges of having to make a more inferential determination (and how to minimize it if possible) are best discussed together, because the question is ultimately one of how to interpret with less than ideal information.

The best solution when a patient refuses a capacity evaluation of course is to persuade the patient to cooperate, if possible, by building rapport or connection with the patient. How best to develop rapport with an uncooperative patient depends on why the patient is refusing. The reason for the patient's behavior is not always obvious, but often there are clues. One of the most common causes of refusal and uncooperative behavior in a hospital is that the patient is angry and resentful for some reason. With such a patient, a confrontational approach is unlikely to work and validating his anger provides the best hope of eliciting cooperation. Whether or not the patient's anger is justified is not the evaluator's concern; the evaluator's task is to make a connection with the patient so a capacity evaluation can be conducted. Angry refusal is a protest, and an important component of this is that the patient does not feel understood. Thus, making the person feel understood—by validating his feelings of anger and resentment—may be the first necessary step to obtaining cooperation. One should express agreement with the patient that it is certainly understandable, given what he has experienced, why he would feel that way. Indeed, one might even say to the patient, given his experience, he has a right to feel that way.

Another reason for refusal may involve fear. An elderly person who fears nursing home placement and has been told by the team that she may be going to one may put up a wall of resistance. For such patients, carefully explaining the purpose of the evaluation and expressing a genuine desire to understand why she believes she can function independently may be the best approach. At other times, the patient's refusal may be based on paranoid delusions, which may or may not be evident.

If attempts at building rapport fail, the evaluator must accept that a certain amount (or perhaps a great deal) of inference will be necessary in order to make a judgment. Although temporizing can be an option (a very good option that should not be forgotten in many situations), sometimes a decision just has to be made. The evaluator's professional role is to make the best judgment based on the available evidence. What cannot be obtained cannot be used, and an important part of the evaluation is documenting the nature of the evidence used for the inference. Often there are various bits of information that can be helpful in drawing informed inferences. These sources include whatever amount of conversation the patient engages in with the evaluator; they may reveal the current mental state of the patient and some of the content of the communication may be informative. Often, reports from the nursing staff and the treatment team can be useful. Reports of observations from outside the hospital can be useful as well.

Some experts have advised that when a patient refuses to be interviewed, the degree of priority given to autonomy can be lessened

6
chapter

INFO

In a patient who is uncooperative with the capacity interview, if attempts to build rapport fail, there is no choice except to infer from the available evidence, perhaps giving additional weight to welfare considerations.

in the overall judgment (Grisso & Appelbaum, 1998; Youngner, 1998). Grisso and Appelbaum, as we saw, advocate a balance scale model in which, under normal circumstances, the scale is skewed in favor of autonomy as a way of reflecting our society's high regard for autonomy. However, they recommend that when a patient refuses a capacity evaluation, the fulcrum can return to the middle. In other words, when one is working with less than ideal information and this is due to the patient's refusal to cooperate, one's welfare-based concerns may need to play a larger role than usual.

This of course increases the likelihood of finding the patient incompetent. And it is likely that such a patient will also disagree with a determination of incapacity, and a more formal determination of capacity will need to be made, that is, by going to court. Even if the patient acquiesces, sometimes the treatment team may decide that they need the approval of a court before proceeding with a treatment in the case of a patient who is not wholly cooperative. Of course, if there are time pressures, then the availability of an emergency court session is an important determining factor regarding whether to wait for a court decision.

Enigmatic Refusals of Highly Beneficial, Low-Risk Treatments

In theory, a competent patient can, at the end of the day, refuse even treatments that are lifesaving with (at least to most observers) relatively little burden. But the capacity evaluator will sometimes encounter a case that presents a true dilemma when the issue is whether the patient is competent.

Consider the following case:

A 24-year-old young man in the emergency room has bacterial meningitis but refuses curative treatment with antibiotics, without which he will die. Despite careful attempts at probing by the treating doctor, the patient cannot state a rationale for his refusal and rejects prolonged discussions. There are no signs of cognitive impairment.

This is a case described by Jonsen, Siegler, and Winslade in their excellent book *Clinical Ethics* (Jonsen et al., 1998, p. 60ff). The difficulty with this case is that the patient *appears* competent; or at least, given the amount of evidence available, there is no obvious reason—aside from his seemingly enigmatic choice—to believe that he lacks the relevant abilities for competence. Yet to honor his refusal is to permit his death, or permit at least a high risk of serious permanent harm. But the intuition against allowing the refusal is very strong.

What can justify such a treatment against a patient's apparently competent wishes? Is it simply old-fashioned paternalism? Given the modern framework for informed consent and patient autonomy, such an override must be supported by a strong rationale for why the patient's competency is in doubt. Current standards of law and ethics do not allow the judgment that "although the patient is making a competent choice, there is a need to override this preference." Thus, one potential interpretation of the situation could be that in an urgent situation with high potential for benefit and with low potential for harm, the threshold for "competence" should be set very high (indeed, maximal) and that this patient's enigmatic refusal does not meet that high standard. After all, the evaluation is truncated by the patient's refusal. And the refusal's rationale is not forthcoming. In an otherwise cognitively intact patient, this lack of rationale is most likely an indication of a missing premise—some underlying factor, perhaps a substantially irrational belief, that is influencing the patient that essentially manifests itself as a lack of reasoning ability.

In this case, it later came to light that the patient's brother had nearly died 12 years ago from an anaphylactic reaction to penicillin. But while in the emergency department, "[the patient] did not, and could not, recall this event and probing did not uncover it ....
[Later] the patient did not recall [his refusal]" (p. 80). In *retrospect*

6
chapter

then, we can say with some degree of confidence that this patient experienced a period of dissociation that impaired his reasoning and appreciation abilities to the point of incapacity. But at the time that the decision had to be made by the treatment providers, this fact of incompetence could not be fully spelled out by the evaluator.

Consider another case:

> A highly educated 65-year-old woman with multiple medical problems, including long-standing diabetes, in the intensive care unit for serious gastrointestinal bleeding is refusing an endoscopic examination to locate the source of bleeding. She is emotionally labile and is anxious. She scores a perfect 30 out of possible 30 on the Mini Mental State examination. When probed about her refusal, she is not able to state a reason and she denies that she wishes to die; in apparent frustration with the continued probing, she finally blurts out in irritation, "It's my body. I get to decide."

One could easily build a case in favor of this patient being judged competent to refuse the diagnostic endoscopy. "It's my body. I get to decide" statement could be taken as providing a type of rationale for her choice. It is not patently false or substantively faulty. Indeed, the combination of both feminist and self-determination undertones of the statement would likely raise a caution flag in the mind of the evaluator who is contemplating overriding this woman's preference. After all, she seems to be simply asserting her rights: she gets to decide and don't ask her so many questions. Further, the results of the bedside mental status test provided positive evidence that her cognition was not grossly compromised; indeed, her cognitive screen score was a perfect score.

It turned out in this case that some amount of temporizing was possible. Although her hematocrit (a measure of blood level in her system) had been dropping steadily over the preceding 12 hours, she was being very closely monitored in the intensive care unit and emergent measures could have been taken in case of sudden deterioration in the patient's clinical status. Indeed, her bleeding did eventually stop. When she was interviewed 2 days later, she revealed something that was quite surprising. When asked why she had refused the endoscopy, she said that at the time she believed that she was in an automotive garage and felt that the doctors were not really doctors but impostors, and she was too afraid to agree to the procedure. When asked, in retrospect, if she had been capable of making the decision to refuse the procedure, she replied, "Are you kidding? I was on a different planet." In fact, she had been delirious with paranoid psychotic symptoms that were hidden from the evaluator. In retrospect, her emotional lability and anxiety were symptoms of an underlying delirium. She was incapacitated because her delusions and hallucinations prevented her from appreciating (believing) what the doctors were telling her. But this information was not available to the capacity evaluator at the time of the evaluation because the very paranoia that caused her incapacity also prevented access to the underlying pathology.

What conclusions ought to be drawn from these cases? Perhaps the main lesson is that these enigmatic refusals *did* exhibit some clues of impairment that needed to be taken very seriously. In both cases, the patients denied that they had a wish to die, but in both cases, they were choosing a course that put them at a high risk of harm in spite of the fact that there were courses of action (antibiotic treatment, endoscopic examination) that were highly beneficial and of low risk. At least on the surface there is a logical tension, if not outright contradiction, in their statements. Grisso and Appelbaum (1998) describe such inconsistencies between one's expressed values ("I don't want to die") and one's treatment choice (choosing the option most likely to risk death) as a potential impairment in the area of reasoning. Such inconsistencies are one important clue to a hidden factor that needs further probing, especially if life is at stake.

Further, at least in the case of the woman with gastrointestinal bleeding, despite her high score on a mental status screen, she did exhibit symptoms consistent with delirium (e.g., significant emotional lability and dysphoria, in addition to the enigmatic refusal). Perhaps the interviewers should have taken this as a clue to perform more in-depth bedside cognitive testing, using more difficult items that, given her education level, she would have been expected to perform well on but which she might have failed given her delirium. This might have given the evaluator more confidence that there may be an underlying brain dysfunction leading to her refusal.

6
chapter

These examples do not imply that all cases of enigmatic refusals are to be treated as cases of "hidden incapacity." That would be far too simplistic. These are cases of patients who in fact were probably not competent to refuse, but whose underlying brain dysfunction-related incapacity was very difficult to discover because the tools at the capacity's evaluator's disposal—the clinical interview and assessment—can sometimes be too insensitive. However, it is important in such cases to focus on subtle clues of incapacity and to make sure that they are explored thoroughly.

The question remains, however, whether an evaluator can infer incapacity based on some undiscovered, underlying impairment (manifesting in these cases as inconsistent reasoning) in such cases, when best efforts at discovery do not yield a clear answer, and the clinical situation is urgent. Note that this is a fundamentally different question than whether the evaluator can use mere disagreement as the basis for incapacity. The following factors speak in its favor: (a) a very high benefit/risk–burden ratio, (b) time urgency, (c) evidence of some underlying psychopathology or brain dysfunction that could very well explain the inconsistent reasoning, and (d) impairment in reasoning ability.

Religious Belief or Delusion?

One of the more common questions asked by trainees is, "How do you know if a psychotic patient's choice (e.g., to refuse a treatment) is due to a religious belief or a delusion?" Assume for a moment that Mr. R is refusing a recommended treatment that is highly beneficial with little burden. He cites a religious reason for his refusal. (We focus on religion because of historical reasons [e.g., case of the Jehovah's Witness] but it is better to see it as just one instance of a more general concept, namely, strongly or deeply held values that influence a person's medical choice.)

When a patient whose decision-making capacity is under question makes a decision based on religious reasons, it can appear as though the capacity evaluator's interpretation has to do with passing judgment on a person's religious belief. But if a capacity evaluation gives the clinician the authority to determine whether a patient's values are "rational," then it seems nothing much is gained by the doctrine of informed consent. Thus it is crucial to apply the appreciation standard correctly in interpreting the situation, by following these steps.

First, the evaluator should assess whether the choice is indeed arising out of a strongly held value that is the patient's. To what extent is the religious belief the *patient's* genuine belief? Is there a reason to believe that the so-called religious belief is not a manifestation of Mr. R's deeply held beliefs and values but rather of a brain dysfunction? For example, suppose Mr. R is refusing life-saving blood transfusions claiming that it is against his religious beliefs. Suppose it turns out that he has never been a member of a religious group that forbids blood transfusions and had already accepted blood transfusions during the same hospitalization, and that there are signs of delirium. In such a case, Mr. R is failing to appreciate his medical situation, because his refusal is based on a belief that is likely due to a brain dysfunction. Another important clue is when the belief is idiosyncratic and is not part of widely accepted understanding of religious belief as a shared cultural system. Thus, a criterion familiar to psychiatrists is the following: "not [a belief] ordinarily accepted by other members of the person's culture or subculture (e.g., it is not an article of religious faith)" (American Psychiatric Association, 1994, p. 765). Even if the patient does belong to a religion, it may be that his beliefs are idiosyncratic and not part of the doctrinal system of that religion.

Of course, all these considerations have to be weighed together. For instance, suppose the patient belongs to a sect that accepts specific, direct revelations from God to its members, and the patient claims that her refusal is based on a direct command from God. The evaluator will need to assess key factors, such as how unusual the belief is within the system (e.g., does it go against another, more highly regarded doctrine?) and how prominent the patient's cognitive or psychiatric impairments appear and the likelihood of the impairment causing the apparently idiosyncratic belief (e.g., perhaps the content of the religious belief is not consistent or changes over time without apparent reason). The focus of the evaluation therefore is not on the rationality of the religious belief itself but rather on whether the evaluator can determine, with a reasonable degree of clinical judgment, that the belief is part of a pathologic process.

6
chapter

Depressed Patients Refusing Beneficial Treatment

Consider a psychiatric inpatient who suffers from a chronic major depressive disorder. His doctors are recommending ECT because, in their estimation based on the patient's history and symptoms, there is a good chance it will help the patient. But the patient refuses ECT saying, "It's not going to help me." At this point, one cannot say the patient's ability to appreciate his situation is diminished. One must first determine: What is the basis for this refusal and is the basis related to some psychiatric condition?

Suppose that over the years, the patient has been treated with a variety of antidepressants, as well as various augmentation and combination approaches. He usually does respond to ECT but the effect lasts only briefly. Upon further questioning, the patient acknowledges this and says, "I don't like the way ECT messes up my memory; it's only going to help me briefly anyway." In this case, he seems to appreciate his condition and the treatment proposed; it may be that, if pressed, he would be able to clarify that in his mind the brief benefit from ECT is outweighed by the side effects. Although on the surface the statement that "It's not going to help me" seems to betray a lack of appreciation, an examination of its basis reveals a set of beliefs that are hard to categorize as "substantially irrational." Clinicians may disagree with those beliefs (and perhaps the arguably correct thing to do clinically is to try to persuade the patient to accept ECT); but this disagreement cannot be the basis to judge this patient incompetent.

On the other hand, imagine that the patient's refusal is based on an obviously defective belief, such as a delusion. For example, his depression may involve a delusion that the doctors are not really doctors at all but demons sent to punish him for his past misdeeds. To the extent that this is an irrational belief that is caused by his depression, leading to the refusal of treatment, the patient lacks the ability to appreciate his situation. This is a relatively easy determination, as long as the delusion can be elicited from the patient.

Less dramatically, the patient could be refusing due to an unshakable nihilism that is sometimes part of severe depressive episodes. Consider a severely depressed patient whose understanding is reasonably intact: He can accurately relay his condition, the nature of the proposed treatment, the likely outcomes of various options, and is even able to appreciate how such treatment might affect him as a matter of likely outcomes (suppose he agrees that ECT in fact would lift him out of the depression). But it is possible that despite all this, there is a failure to "value" the treatment because of a relentless hopelessness. He may state that "it's a waste of time treating someone like me" because he is "totally worthless" and because he "deserves to die."

Some have argued that the current model of assessing capacity may miss this more "affective" aspect of capacity, as discussed in chapter 2. But an evaluator should interpret such a situation much in the same way we view a patient with a delusional religious belief, as above: (a) the self-punishing belief is not part of her actual value system and (b) we can explain where it comes from, viz., psychopathology of depression. Thus, the appreciation standard, correctly interpreted, can show that such a patient is indeed incompetent. Of course, there may not be a bright line that can always be drawn. This is why a judgment is needed. But such nihilism, if determined to be essentially a manifestation of depression, may constitute a substantially irrational belief.

When the depressed patient also has a serious medical illness, the assessment can become particularly difficult. Suppose the illness is life threatening and chronic, and requires burdensome treatment, for example, ventilator support or long-term hemodialysis (Cohen, Dobscha, Hails, Pekow, & Chochinov, 2002). Is the refusal of treatment a manifestation of the depressive disorder? Or is it a considered and evolving response, reflecting a thoughtful and adaptive acceptance of one's own mortality? The assessment of the "authenticity" of the patient's choice of forgoing life-sustaining treatment can be very difficult to assess in such cases. Some have found that treatment of elderly depressed patients changes their end-of-life treatment preferences (Ganzini, Lee, Heintz, Bloom, & Fenn, 1994). On the other hand, although depression can certainly affect capacity in some patients, most remain competent even with depression (Appelbaum et al., 1999; Grisso & Appelbaum, 1995). Depression rates among those who die after cessation of dialysis treatment appear no different than the overall rate of depression in that population (Cohen et al., 2002). What these data show is that the mere fact of a patient's depression does not imply that the patient who refuses life-sustaining treatment is incompetent.

The capacity evaluator's difficult task is therefore to assess whether in a particular case, the patient's depression (or other condition) is compromising his decision-making capacity. The framework for such an evaluation is no different than that discussed already. But there are some additional factors or questions that may help guide the evaluation. The assessment should take into account the patient's previously stated wishes (or value system), the facts of the patient's illness (e.g., a depressed patient who is an excellent transplant candidate and is high on the transplant list versus a patient on chronic dialysis with increasing burdens and side effects and other serious complications), and the quality of the reasoning process expressed by the patient ("I feel trapped; there's no other choice that I can see" versus "I've benefited from dialysis over the years but now I think it's just getting to be too burdensome"). The clinician's own bias must also be carefully explored in the interpretation of the situation. The clinician's bias—whether it be excessive protectionism or an overeager acceptance of "self-determination"—does not serve the patient well.

Documentation of Capacity Evaluation and Determination

Documentation of the capacity evaluation serves several functions. The most important purpose is to justify and explain the rationale for the capacity judgment. A determination of capacity is a normative judgment, and it must be explicitly justified with evidence and reasoning. Such a document then helps the treatment team make their own decisions, and can be further used, if necessary, in court proceedings.

Documentation also serves an educational function regarding what a capacity evaluation is, what standards are operative in the hospital (or the jurisdiction), and how determinations are justified in relation to the context and the performance of the patient. The educational function may be particularly important because, as discussed in chapter 3, a survey of health professionals who routinely conduct capacity consultations report that health care providers who consult them fail to understand the decision-specific nature of capacity judgments and that these providers also often fail to provide sufficient disclosure to patients when obtaining informed consent (Ganzini et al., 2003).

The list in Table 6.1 adapted from Grisso and Appelbaum (1998) is a useful guide for what to include in a documentation of a capacity assessment.

Table 6.1 | Recommendations for Documentation

- A statement of why and by whom the consultation was requested, for which medical treatment or procedure.
- A notation that the patient was informed about the purpose of the evaluation and a description of the patient's response.
- A brief review of the patient's mental status at the time of the evaluation.
- A description of the information that was conveyed to the patient about the treatment choice, including the identity of the person who undertook the disclosure.
- Information regarding the patient's performance on the relevant standards for decisional competence (which may vary across jurisdictions), with findings of impaired abilities explained by its cognitive, medical, or psychiatric basis.
- A description of the potential consequences of the patient's choice.
- An analysis of the balancing process in which the evaluator weighed the relative importance of the interests in decisional autonomy and protection of the patient.
- A statement regarding the clinician's opinion concerning the patient's competence.
- A statement outlining the scope of the finding. When the patient is determined to be incompetent, specify the decision at issue, and note that the finding does not extend to other decisions.

6
chapter

Note: Adapted from *Assessing Competence to Consent to Treatment: A Guide for Physicians and Other Health Professionals*, by T. Grisso and P. S. Appelbaum, 1998 New York: Oxford University Press. Copyright 1998 by Oxford University Press.

The recommendation (Grisso & Appelbaum, 1998) that the capacity determination be phrased so as to reflect the fact that the clinician is approximating an ideal court's decision is a good one. Thus, in summarizing one's assessment, one should state, "In my opinion, a court would find the patient lacking the capacity to. . . ." Of course, there is no legal requirement that an evaluator's judgment be stated this way. However, it reinforces for the capacity evaluator and for the treatment team two important points: that the judgment is meant to reflect societal values as embodied in the legal system and that such judgments can be overridden by a court of law.

After the Assessment | 7

The capacity evaluator's role as a consultant will sometimes extend beyond rendering a judgment about a patient's consent capacity. If the patient has been deemed incapable of making her own decision, there may be questions about *surrogate decision making*. When there is a close and caring family member involved, the transition to surrogate decision making is usually straightforward and the consultant will not need to be involved. However, there are instances in which understanding the legal and ethical limits and the bases for surrogate decision making is essential in helping the treatment team manage the case. This chapter first discusses surrogate decision making for persons with and without advance directives in the medical setting. The next section then briefly discusses psychiatric advance directives, as there are special issues for surrogate decision making in the psychiatric context. The following section then discusses the variety of situations in which going to court is the best or only solution.

Finally, sometimes even when the patient's decision-making capacity is intact, the capacity evaluator may need to play an additional role beyond simply dispensing a judgment about capacity. This chapter closes with a brief discussion of how to engage competent patients to help them make difficult decisions. The need to maintain a clinical perspective during and after the capacity evaluation is emphasized.

Surrogate Decision Making for Most Medical Treatment Decisions

We recently analyzed data from a national panel survey of older Americans (Juster & Suzman, 1995), examining 3,746 deaths of those in the panel over the age of 60 during the period from 2002 to 2006 (Silveira, Kim, & Langa, 2009), representative of deaths in that age group in the United States. Forty percent died in a hospital, 20% died in a nursing home, and only a few died in hospice (6%). Approximately 42% of deaths required some type of decision making about life-sustaining treatment prior to death. Of those, 70% of patients were unable to make those decisions themselves. Thus, surrogate medical decision making at the end of life is very common.

In some of these cases, the treatment teams may turn to the capacity evaluator to help facilitate surrogate decision making, especially if the evaluator has already been involved in determining the decisional capacity of the patient and has begun to develop a relationship with the family and others connected to the patient. There may in addition be disagreement, or even conflict, among family members or between the family and the treatment team, that may have triggered a request for help from the treatment team.

Decision making for an incapacitated patient can be divided into two broad types of situations: when some type of formal advance care planning has taken place versus when there has not. Advance care planning falls into two types of mechanisms: the *instructional health care directive* (also often called the living will) and *proxy advance directive* (as health care proxies or as durable power of attorney for health care). All states have some type of advance directive statutes, and most have provisions for both types (American Bar Association, 2008a).

When There Is an Advance Directive

INSTRUCTIONAL DIRECTIVES

Instructional health care directives, sometimes called the living will, record the explicit treatment preferences of the patients. They can vary in complexity and specificity. Usually the directives address end-of-life decision making. Those who complete instructional directives anticipate potential future situations of incapacity, and express their preference regarding life-sustaining treatment. About 45% of recent decedents, representative of U.S. population over age

60, had completed a living will by the time of death. Compared to those who did not fill out a living will, the completers were more likely to be older, White, and educated. About 90% of living wills are written by people who want to limit end-of-life care (Silveira et al., 2009).

Although theoretically a highly attractive idea—with its promise of extending the autonomy of the patient even when the patient becomes incapacitated—the instructional directive has come under considerable criticism over the years. A review of living wills found that there are substantive limitations to the living will as a social policy instrument (Fagerlin & Schneider, 2004). Although the completion rates are higher in those who are seriously ill, most people do not complete living wills. Even if people do fill out a living will, they may not know what they want, given the complexity of medical decisions. Also, even if they do know what they want, describing and anticipating the unknown future can be a daunting task, whether it be about what might happen to them, but also in regard to people's own changes in preferences over time. Further, an instructional directive must still be available and interpreted by the medical team and, more commonly, by the patient's surrogates. All of this is not to deny that living wills can sometimes be extremely helpful, especially when a patient already has a terminal illness with a predictable course and has anticipated key decision points and has been able to discuss and document his treatment preferences. However, in most cases, most of the decision making for an incapacitated person must still rest on a third party who has to exercise some degree of judgment.

Because of these limitations of the instructional directive, there has been some movement to recognize its limits and to accommodate this limit into policy. For example, a recent Maryland statute gives the patient the option of designating whether the living will is meant to be binding or to be used as guidance with some flexibility by using language such as, "I authorize them to be flexible in applying these statements if they feel that doing so would be in my best interest." Of course, the patient can also choose to designate the following: "I realize I cannot foresee everything that might happen after I can no longer decide for myself. Still, I want whoever is making decisions on my behalf and my health care providers to follow my stated preferences exactly as written, even if they think that some alternative is better" (Maryland, 2007).

PROXY DIRECTIVES

An advance directive, rather than or in addition to an instructional directive, can appoint a proxy who can take on the role of a substitute decision maker when the patient becomes incapacitated. Such proxy directives are more popular than living wills. Among decedents aged 60 and over who died between 2002 and 2006 in the United States, half (54%) had a proxy directive (Silveira et al., 2009). The obvious advantage of a proxy over an instructional directive is that the details of the future need not be anticipated in detail. It can also be combined with an instructional directive to help guide the proxy decision maker. The proxy can take in the relevant information at the time that the decision needs to be made, and do her best to represent the patient's preferences (see later in this chapter). Thus, this mechanism works best if the patient communicates his preferences and values to the proxy.

Almost every state in the United States has an advance directive law that allows the appointment of proxy decision makers. Many states have a combined directive that contains both a proxy directive and an instructional directive. Laws providing for proxies do vary however. For most medical treatment decisions during a general hospital admission, the proxy has the authority to make decisions just as a patient would. But there are some exceptions. For example, most health care proxies cannot authorize psychiatric admissions, ECT, sterilization, abortion, or psychosurgery. Also, proxies generally cannot override the dissent of incompetent but still verbal patients. These special cases are discussed below.

When There Are No Advance Directives

Many, if not most, people still do not complete an advance directive, even for end-of-life decisions. For treatment decisions that are not about end-of-life care, it is likely that formal advance directives are even less common. Thus, in most instances of decision making for an incapacitated patient, the surrogate decision maker is not a previously designated person. Turning to the de facto surrogate decision maker (traditionally "next of kin") has a long and respected tradition in medicine and this tradition has been formalized in specific laws in most states. As of January 2008, 43 states and Washington, DC, had at least some form of de facto surrogate treatment decision-making law that explicitly gives decision-making authority to family members (and, rarely, to other close associates; American Bar Association, 2008b).

These laws provide legal clarity to what has been practice based on custom. They usually also spell out the hierarchy of authority that can be useful when there is a disagreement among available surrogates. The order is almost always spouse, adult child, parent, sibling, then usually next nearest relative, but sometimes a close friend. Some states explicitly mention life partners or "long-term spouse-like relationships" as taking precedence over even an adult child, taking the place of "spouse" in the traditional hierarchy of surrogates (e.g., New Mexico; American Bar Association, 2008b). But this varies. For example, in Arizona, a "domestic partner" has precedence over a sibling but not above a parent or adult child. One argument for completing an explicit advance directive is precisely to allow some patients to appoint someone who may not be recognized by the surrogate treatment laws.

Although surrogate treatment laws provide clarity to those states that have them, one cannot infer that the absence of such laws implies a prohibition of the practice of de facto surrogate decision making. Some states do not have such a law at all (Massachusetts, Minnesota, Missouri, Nebraska, New Hampshire, Rhode Island, and Vermont) and others have a law that is limited in scope (e.g., some laws address only do-not-resuscitate orders or other end-of-life situations, others do not apply to decisions to withdraw nutrition and hydration, others exclude certain types of psychiatric interventions, other states only have laws regulating medical research surrogates). It is a reasonable presumption that even when specific surrogate treatment laws do not exist, family surrogates generally will play the role of decision makers for their incapacitated relatives. But consultants should familiarize themselves with the limitations and exceptions for such a presumption in their own jurisdiction by consulting with the hospital's counsel.

7
chapter

Decision-Making Standards for Substitute Decision Makers

When an appropriate surrogate decision maker is present (either a previously appointed proxy, or a de facto surrogate specified in statute, or a next of kin in states without surrogate treatment laws), what is the standard that such a surrogate should use to make her decision about the patient's treatment? Given the priority accorded to patient autonomy, there is a natural hierarchy regarding how a treatment decision should be made for an incapacitated patient: (a) previously stated specific preferences, (b) substituted judgment, and (c) best interests. These standards reflect both provisions in statutes (i.e., from state health care proxy or durable power of attorney [DPOA] statutes) and consensus in the literature on surrogate decision making.

PREVIOUSLY STATED PREFERENCE

The ideal situation is when a patient has expressed his informed preferences regarding specific treatments for specific clinical situations, preferably in a written document, in addition to discussions with his doctors and family. This can happen if the patient and the family can anticipate the type of situations that can occur (e.g., an end-stage cancer patient) so that the "advance" portion is not so far into the future. Unfortunately, for the reasons discussed above regarding living wills, this is not as frequent an occurrence as one might wish for. In most situations, one therefore has to rely on either the *substituted judgment standard* or the *best interests standard*.

SUBSTITUTED JUDGMENT

When the patient's specific preference for a given clinical situation is not clear, then most states require use of the substituted judgment standard by the surrogate decision maker. This standard asks: If this incompetent patient were in fact competent, what would she choose to do in this situation? Sometimes this is called the "probable wishes" standard, as distinguished from the actual wishes standard (i.e., a directly relevant instructional directive or the actual previously stated preference mentioned above; Meisel, 1998). The notion of "probable" wishes is an important point to keep in mind, because the standard requires that a reasoned inference be made, recognizing that the actual preferences are not known. From a theoretical point of view, the goal would be such that "what the patient would have wanted" and what the surrogate chooses for the patient perfectly coincides.

Of course, there is an element of metaphysical impossibility in validating this, because that would require knowledge of what the patient would have wanted *now* were he competent, which is something that cannot be known. This is why studies of concordance between patient and surrogate preferences—if they are eliciting concurrent preferences—must use hypothetical decision-making scenarios. The most comprehensive and up-to-date review of all relevant studies on the accuracy of surrogate substitute decision making shows that surrogates and patients agree about 68% of the time (Shalowitz, Garrett-Mayer, & Wendler, 2006).

In these studies, the accuracy is not affected by the mode of designation of the surrogate; surrogates selected by patients are no more accurate than those "selected" according to state statutes, probably because there is such a large overlap between the two types of designations. Also, preponderance of evidence on the effect of prior discussion of the patient's treatment preferences on the accuracy of surrogate decisions shows no significant effect (Shalowitz et al., 2006). Most of these studies tended to focus on decisions regarding life-sustaining treatment. One factor that seems to increase accuracy of the surrogate's decisions is if the decision-making situation is relevant to the patients' current health state. This suggests that the 68% accuracy rate is probably an underestimate for real-life situations, if in real life patients discuss their preferences close to the time of their eventual incapacity (because the 68% accuracy mostly refers to studies that used hypothetical scenarios).

The fact that nearly a third of the hypothetical decisions made by surrogates do not match the preferences of the patients should be tempered by a couple of points. First, the issue of "accuracy" assumes that there is a nonmoving target, that there is a robust intraperson stability in health care choices. But in fact a substantial

7
chapter

proportion of patients change their minds regarding life-sustaining interventions; up to half initially accepting then decline such an intervention (Emanuel, Emanuel, Stoeckle, Hummel, & Barry, 1994). A recent study of 818 physicians comparing their end-of-life treatment preferences given in two surveys (3 years apart) found that one in five subjects who desired least aggressive treatment changed their mind, and only two in five who had initially desired aggressive treatment maintained that preference. Persons without an advance directive were more than twice as likely to change their minds (Wittink et al., 2008). Second, the value of appointing a proxy may be broader than simply seeking an "accurate" decision. In one study of dialysis patients, the patients were asked how much leeway they would be willing to grant their surrogate decision makers to "override their advance directive if overriding were in their best interests," in the event of their own future incapacity due to a dementing illness. Thirty-one percent were wiling to grant "complete leeway" and 11% "a lot of leeway" (Sehgal et al., 1992). Thus, over 4 out of 10 patients placed a tremendous amount of trust in their surrogates—even to override their stated preferences, depending on what the future brings.

Surrogates and doctors should also take some comfort in the fact that despite the individualistic autonomy framework behind the substituted judgment standard, most terminally ill patients prefer some combination of their own preferences (in the form of substituted judgment) and the views of their loved ones or physicians (Nolan et al., 2005).

BEST INTERESTS

Even if the patient's probable wishes in a situation are not known or not knowable, the need for the decision still exists. Often, it is not clear what the patient's "probable" wishes would have been and it would be too speculative to attribute a preference to the patient. The decision cannot be arbitrary and some standard must be used. The standard of last resort, at least for previously competent adults, is the best interests standard. This standard simply says that the decision should be made based on weighing the potential benefits against the risk of harm or the amount of burden involved in the proposed treatment(s).

Although simply stated, there are some limitations to the best interests standard. The most obvious is that people have different views about what is best for a patient. Some have advocated a view that treatments that sustain certain types of human existence (e.g., permanent unconsciousness, or dependence on intensive medical care) should be considered "futile" and can be discontinued or not offered even without patient or surrogate consent (Schneiderman et al., 1990). On the other hand, not everyone would support this type of unilateral action based on quality of life. As one court has noted, the use of the best interests standard must not creep over into "assessments of the personal worth or social utility of another's life, or the value of that life to others" (In re Conroy, 1984).

Despite these caveats, the best interests standard remains an important standard with considerable support and justification by prominent commissions and case law (In re Conroy, 1984; President's Commission, 1982), even to allow withholding or withdrawing life-sustaining treatment, based on considerations of net burdens and benefits of treatment.

COMBINATION STANDARDS

As noted above, sometimes even in legal definitions the standards for substitute decision making are not cleanly divided between the best interests and the substituted judgment standard. For instance, the recent Mental Capacity Act (2005) of England and Wales explicitly requires a best interests basis for surrogate decision making. But its definition of best interests includes "(a) the person's past and present wishes and feelings (and, in particular, any relevant written statement made by him when he had capacity), (b) the beliefs and values that would be likely to influence his decision if he had capacity, and (c) the other factors that he would be likely to consider if he were able to do so." Obviously, one should not simply assume the term "best interests" has a uniform meaning, and anyone assisting surrogates in their decision making should be aware of the standards applicable in her jurisdiction.

From a practical point of view, the reality is that most patients want their medical decisions to be some combination of their own preferences and the recommendations or expertise of their

7
chapter

physicians. A recent longitudinal study of patients with cancer, heart failure, or amyotrophic lateral sclerosis (Lou Gehrig's disease) found that such a preference for shared decision making was fairly stable (Sulmasy et al., 2007).

Psychiatric Advance Directives

As we saw in chapter 3, the loss of treatment consent capacity is common among psychiatric inpatients (Okai et al., 2007; Owen et al., 2008). Persons with serious mental disorders whose exacerbations can lead to hospitalizations and loss of decisional capacity may benefit from the use of psychiatric advance directives. Although psychiatric advance directives are becoming more common, their use can differ from traditional medical advance directives and a brief discussion will be useful.

General Information

Psychiatric advance directives are best thought of as part of overall, long-term treatment plans for patients with serious, chronic psychiatric illnesses such as schizophrenia or bipolar disorder. As crisis or exacerbation management plans, they can sensitively incorporate the unique treatment response history or preferences of the patient. Thus, their use arises in contexts (e.g., mental health clinics or psychiatric hospitals) that generally do not require special consultations for capacity assessment; it is likely that a clinician will face the issue of a psychiatric advance directive more often in his role as a provider of psychiatric care, rather than in his role as a capacity consultant.

Psychiatric advance directives can be used to document the mental health treatment preferences regarding the use of psychotropic medications, somatic therapies such as ECT, hospitalization, special strategies in treatment, including, in some cases, refusals of certain types of treatment. It can also be used to designate a surrogate decision maker. Such directives can be useful when a patient is not capable of consenting to certain psychiatric treatments, because the treatment team can provide the needed care without having to go to court. Also, when providers and patients plan together strategies for crisis management using psychiatric advance directives, it may improve the therapeutic alliance and improve the patient's understanding of the relevant issues regarding treatment (Elbogen et al., 2007; Swanson, McCrary, Swartz, Elbogen, & Van Dorn, 2006a).

INFO

An excellent resource is the National Resource Center on Psychiatric Advance Directives (http://www.nrc-pad.org).

A psychiatric advance directive can also include the familiar elements of a medical advance directive, regarding medical treatment preferences for a psychiatric patient who is at higher risk for becoming incapacitated for making medical treatment decisions. For these and other reasons, there have been considerable efforts by various groups to increase the use of such directives.

Some Specific Issues Regarding Psychiatric Advance Directives

Like most advance directives, the degree of interest is greater than the actual completion rates. Although a majority of psychiatric outpatients express an interest in completing a psychiatric advance directive, a recent survey of patients in five U.S. cities showed that about 4–13% of patients have completed such a directive (Swanson et al., 2006b). As noted above, there is good evidence that clinician–patient collaboration, in the form of facilitated completion of directives, increases completion rates, understanding, and satisfaction.

About half of the states have specific statutes providing for psychiatric advance directives, and in all other states, patients can use existing medical advance directive mechanisms (such as durable power of attorney for health care or health care proxy laws) to create a psychiatric advance directive. Because of the variety of ways in which the laws are written, it is important to know specific provisions of that state. Some points that are particularly relevant for clinical decision making are as follows, and a clinician should become familiar with the specific situation in her jurisdiction.

First, although a general health care proxy's authority does not usually extend to "special treatment" decisions such as for ECT,

7
chapter

psychotropic medications, and psychiatric hospitalizations, a specific psychiatric advance directive statute can broaden the authority of the health care proxy (if specified by the patient) to include such decisions. Second, in many states with psychiatric advance directive laws, the patient's capacity status need not be determined by the court before the initiation of treatment under the directive; in most states, the determination of the patient's treatment consent capacity by the treating clinician will be sufficient. Third, it appears that patients can write "Ulysses contracts." That is, it is possible to write psychiatric advance directives in most states that would allow treatment providers, in accordance with the directive, to override the patient's wishes at the time of the crisis or exacerbation (Henderson, Swanson, Szmukler, Thornicroft, & Zinkler, 2008). However, some recent state laws do not allow such Ulysses contracts (New Jersey and Washington).

Fourth, and perhaps most controversial, there is a worry among some clinicians that a psychiatric advance directive might be used to prohibit treatments that are deemed necessary by the treating clinicians (Srebnik, Appelbaum, & Russo, 2004). Psychiatric advance directives do not override the prevailing dangerousness standard for involuntary psychiatric admissions. Consider a patient with a psychiatric advance directive that refuses all treatments is involuntarily admitted to a psychiatric hospital. If such a directive cannot be overridden, then the hospital will be faced with a patient whom it can "neither treat nor discharge" (Appelbaum, 2004). Significant proportion of clinicians when surveyed state that they would not honor "no treatment" advance directives, with the proportion being much higher if the reason for the refusal is a delusion (Wilder, Elbogen, Swartz, Swanson, & Van Dorn, 2007). Currently, specific psychiatric advance directive laws do not require clinicians to follow directive instructions that conflict with emergency care, that are unfeasible, that would prevent involuntary commitment, or that conflict with "community practice standards" (Swanson et al., 2006a). But the status of some of these "override" clauses remains uncertain, given the Second Circuit Court's decision in *Hargrave v. Vermont*, which found a Vermont "override" law inconsistent with the federal American with Disabilities Act (Appelbaum, 2004; Swanson et al., 2006a).

In summary, a psychiatric advance directive is a potentially powerful tool of collaboration between patients and their clinicians to enhance their treatment while at the same time (and perhaps by means of) enhancing their voice in what kind of treatments they receive during the most vulnerable periods of their illnesses. There is a great desire among patients and a general acceptance by clinicians, and most states make provisions for such directives. However, there are important variations among jurisdictions that must be taken into account in practice as well as unsettled issues that inevitably arise when one attempts to pin down the scope of specific future decisions.

Going to Court

Although the majority of treatment consent capacity evaluations in the general hospital setting are directly incorporated into medical decision making for the patient, some cases do need to go to court.

Inability to Care for Oneself

In the general hospital setting, perhaps the most common reason for going to court is when an elderly patient who had been living alone but no longer can do so safely needs to be placed in a living facility. For example, a patient with progressing dementia who had been managing with the help of a spouse—indeed, whose level of disability had been masked by the efforts of the spouse—may suddenly appear to deteriorate when the spouse dies, and can no longer manage alone. For such persons, the general hospital often serves as a social transition point from independent to dependent living. What may begin as an admission for an exacerbation of a chronic illness (due to forgetting to take medications), or an apparently minor problem (e.g., urinary tract infection) with changes in mental status, eventually becomes a guardianship issue. For a patient who clearly is incompetent and who insists on going back home to an unsafe environment, there may be no choice but to go

7
chapter

to court. Ideally, a caring family member would petition to become the patient's guardian. But if the patient has no family members, or lacks the financial means to hire an attorney, sometimes a hospital may need to petition the courts for a guardian. The capacity evaluator needs to be aware of the specific laws and procedures when the capacity determination involves the capacity to decide about one's place of residence, as this often engages a state's specific statutes regarding guardianship.

Special Medical Treatments or Procedures

Some medical interventions are controversial because there is the specter of exposing the patient to some risk, burden, harm, or indignity, not for the sake of the patient's welfare or preference, but because it could serve someone else's interests. For psychiatric interventions—such as antipsychotics, ECT, and psychosurgery—a primary concern has been the issue of using medical procedures for social control. In many states, the basis for involuntary admission to a psychiatric hospital (usually based on considerations of welfare to the patient and those affected by him) is different from the basis for involuntary treatment with psychotropic medications or ECT (which usually hinges on the patient's incapacity to make medical decisions). In such states, an involuntarily admitted patient who refuses treatment can only be treated against her will if a court decides that the patient is incompetent (Appelbaum, 1994).

In the case of psychosurgery, thousands of patients, primarily housed in long-term facilities, were exposed to what amounted to unregulated neurosurgical experimentation from 1930s through the 1950s until the advent of antipsychotic medications (Valenstein, 1986). There has been a resurgence of interest in different types of psychosurgery in recent years, with particular interest in deep brain stimulation for treatment refractory depression (Mayberg et al., 2005) but also for a variety of conditions including addictions, aggressive behavioral disorders, and even anorexia nervosa (Elias & Cosgrove, 2008). In the treatment setting, most states currently prohibit psychosurgery involving incompetent patients, or allow it based only on court approval. In the research setting, unlike the unregulated abuses of the early 20th century, now any psychosurgery that is experimental must be approved by a research ethics review board (called Institutional Review Boards or IRBs in the United States) and the patient-subject must give informed consent. Some states have recently enacted laws that would appear to specifically prohibit surrogate consent for psychosurgical experiments (Code of Virginia, 2002).

Another "extraordinary" intervention with a history of spectacular abuses is sterilization. In the early 20th century, sterilization was widely advocated as part of the eugenics movement. In fact, the famous jurist Oliver Wendell Holmes in his 1927 majority opinion in *Buck v. Bell* justified sterilization with the opinion that "three generations of imbeciles are enough" (Lombardo, 2008). Women felt to be mentally retarded or psychiatrically ill or in prisons were sterilized without consent (Committee on Bioethics, 1999; Dubler & White, 1995). It is estimated that about 60,000 persons were sterilized in the United States during this period (Reilly, 1991). Today, sterilization of mentally incompetent persons requires court approval, and professional societies have adopted thoughtful guidelines (Committee on Bioethics, 1999).

Patient Disagrees With Surrogate or With Determination by Clinician

Another situation in which it is necessary to go to court is when an incompetent person disagrees with his surrogate's decision or with a capacity evaluator's determination that the patient is incompetent. This is true even if the patient's surrogate is explicitly designated in an advance proxy directive. Most health care proxy laws do not authorize a proxy to override the active objection of a patient, even if that patient has been deemed incapacitated by a physician who has conducted a formal capacity evaluation.

Surrogate Not Available, Unqualified, or in Conflict

If a medical intervention has very high benefit-to-risk ratio but is quite invasive—say, a relatively urgent neurosurgical procedure—then it will be a judgment call as to whether an emergency court hearing is necessary or not, especially if the patient is awake and conversant (albeit confused and delirious) and is refusing the

7
chapter

procedure. Sometimes there is no clear line between an emergency (in which one would proceed with an exception to informed consent justification) and a situation in which an urgent court hearing is the best option. In general, factors that would favor proceeding to court include (a) the lack of a family surrogate or a health care proxy, (b) the availability of urgent court hearing in the jurisdiction, (c) the relative invasiveness of the procedure, and (d) the benefit-to-risk ratio is not clear-cut in favor of the intervention.

Sometimes cases go to court because the team believes that the surrogate decision maker is not able to carry out her duties—whether this person be a de facto surrogate, a health care proxy or durable power of attorney for health care, or even a guardian. For example, an elderly spouse with signs of dementia or cognitive impairment may not be able to make decisions as a surrogate. Old age is the strongest risk factor for AD, for instance, and a certain percentage of the elderly spouses of incapacitated elderly people will themselves be quite impaired. Sometimes the surrogate decision maker may fail in his role by doing something that is against the clearly stated wishes of the patient or, when information for substituted judgment is lacking, doing what is obviously not in the interests of the patient, perhaps for the surrogate's personal gain.

When there are intractable conflicts among the potential surrogates, courts may have to decide who will have the final decision-making authority for the patient. For patients without a formally designated surrogate such as a health care proxy, it was noted above that most states have some type of de facto surrogate treatment laws, and even if such laws do not exist, there is a strong tradition of turning to the "next of kin" as the rightful surrogate decision maker. Many surrogate treatment laws that designate surrogates provide a hierarchy. However, there may be conflicts that still need to go to court (e.g., when two people of same priority, such as two adult children, disagree).

Another situation in which a guardianship should be sought is when other mechanisms for surrogate decision making are not available for an incapacitated patient who is likely to face a series of major medical decisions. For example, one occasionally runs into the following type of situation. A long-time resident of a residential state psychiatric facility (or perhaps a facility for mentally handicapped adults) is admitted to a general hospital with a newly diagnosed cancer. The patient may have no family and is without a guardian. Suppose the patient's prognosis is not dismal (say, 60% chance of cure, with good quality of life upon recovery) but the treatments may be burdensome, lengthy, and quite uncomfortable. For a patient such as this, there will be not only the question of whether to proceed with the burdensome treatment, but also a series of important medical decisions that will need to be made in the future. It does not serve the patient well if one has to engage a slow administrative or legal process for each future decision. The best scenario for a patient like this is to have an experienced guardian who can work closely with the treatment team across time, as well as with others such as the hospital's ethics committee or ethics consultants. Unfortunately, guardianship laws and resources vary by state, and sometimes the treatment team may need to be proactive in ensuring that there is a legally authorized decision maker who can look out for the patient's best interests.

A slight variation on the above case is more common, namely, the very ill intensive care unit (ICU) patient who is incapacitated and without a surrogate decision maker (White et al., 2007). In a recent study of seven medical centers (East and West coast centers), 5.5% (range: 0–27%) of all ICU deaths occurred in persons without capacity and without surrogates. In 81% of the cases, the decision to limit life-sustaining treatment was made by the ICU team or in consultation with another physician, and in 97% without judicial review as recommended by most major medical societies (White et al., 2007). No doubt this will remain an area of continuing legal and clinical controversy.

It should be noted that the case of an incompetent patient with no available surrogate is mentioned in some surrogate treatment laws that provide for a process without involving the courts. For example, the Arizona law explicitly allows health care providers to make decisions on behalf of such patients in consultation with the hospital's ethics committee. When the committee is not available, the treating physician must consult a second physician, and their consensus allows the treating team to make the decisions. In New York, DNR (do not resuscitate) orders may be written for such patients if two physicians concur that resuscitation is "medically futile." But the legal situation varies by state. Obviously, one must be educated about laws in one's jurisdiction regarding these matters, and also about the established practices in interpreting such statutes in one's own institution.

Competent Patients Facing Difficult Decisions

In a book on the assessment of treatment consent capacity, it may seem out of place to have a section, even if brief, on working with competent patients. After all, isn't the capacity evaluator's job finished once the capacity determination is made and communicated to the consulting team, especially when the patient is competent? I noted earlier that the evaluation of treatment consent capacity needs to be considered from the clinical standpoint, not just the legal standpoint. The approach endorsed in this book is that treatment consent capacity determination—unlike other more clearly "forensic" evaluations—is one part of an overall clinical problem. The capacity evaluator should not take off her clinician's hat during (and after) a capacity evaluation.

Varieties of Autonomy

The concept of autonomy has taken a dominant place in modern medicine and medical ethics (Schneider, 1998). The term is often intuitively equated with concepts such as right to self-determination, right to choose, freedom from paternalism, and other related concepts. Although it has a variety of technical uses in philosophical theory, it is probably most commonly used in modern medicine to denote the independence of an individual's decision making (Manson & O'Neill, 2007). When the term is used to explain the authority of the patient that takes precedence over the paternalism of physicians, it has an adversarial, boundary-drawing character. When this notion of independence is carried to an extreme, the burden of autonomy can be *imposed* on patients, as a kind of "mandatory autonomy" (Schneider, 1998). Understood within this highly individualistic framework that is now dominant in bioethics, it is not difficult to see why even a clinician may take his role to be finished once a capacity determination is made: the patient is competent and she must be left alone to decide what she wants. After all, isn't the right to self-determination in medical decisions "about as absolute a right" as one sees in law (Meisel, 1998)?

Yet a clinician must be careful not to conflate respecting a competent patient's right to refuse treatment with the limits of his professional obligation. To do so is to risk abandoning the patient to her rights. Between coercion and abandonment lies a large space that cannot be ignored because that is precisely the space within which the clinician must work. Failure to see this space, and to engage the patient within it, results from a false dichotomy created by a legalistic and adversarial view of patient autonomy: the paternalistic doctor must be kept at bay, so that the patient can exercise her right to choose. But within the patient's right to choose, the physician can still engage the patient without imposing his own will. One might say that the physician must use a conception of autonomy that recognizes this space, which we might call "autonomy at the bedside" (Kim & Cist, 2004).

Autonomy at the Bedside

Suppose that a competent patient is refusing an intervention that is low risk, with a high potential benefit—the sort of treatment that would be accepted by most patients. It is true that at the end of the day, if the patient is competent, the clinician's legal limits are clear: the patient's choice must be respected. But in a clinical sense, respecting and promoting patient self-determination requires more than simply doing whatever the patient wants, and to ensure that what the patient wants is what he truly desires. A patient whose severe pain is undertreated may wish to die by refusing the treatment, but one would hardly think that such a preference is a *considered* preference. The idea is to remove at least the most obvious obstacles to good decision making. Some of these are within the control of the clinician to address and they are discussed briefly here.

First, are the patient's most bothersome symptoms being adequately managed? Pain management is an obvious issue but other symptoms like nausea, shortness of breath, insomnia, and constipation,

BEST PRACTICE

Even if a patient is competent, be sure to address obstacles to good decision making, such as

- pain and other burdensome symptoms
- psychiatric conditions
- misunderstandings due to cultural, social role, or power differences between patients and the treatment team

among others, can be quite burdensome to a seriously ill patient having to face a major medical decision.

Second, there are often prominent psychiatric conditions that go untreated or unaddressed. Major depression is an obvious example. It may be easy to overlook depression because many of its symptoms (fatigue, poor sleep, low appetite, lack of motivation, etc.) are common to serious medical illnesses. Uncertainties of the medical situation can cause paralyzing anxiety in some. Persons with substance abuse with medical problems causing pain are at risk for undertreatment of their pain, often leading to conflict between the patient and the treatment team. There are patients who are easily overwhelmed or whose coping style (or the lack of it) can place inordinate interpersonal burdens on the treatment team. Patients with personality disorders who feel helpless or angry in their situation can quickly make the treatment team feel helpless (and angry) too. Such patients seem to behave in inexplicably self-destructive and/or antagonizing ways, and the treatment team will often need help from a psychiatric consultant to help manage the situation.

Third, sometimes even in the absence of psychiatric conditions and burdensome symptoms, there may be a certain amount of misunderstanding between the treatment team and the patient that may go unrecognized. These could be due to barriers of culture and socioeconomic status, or issues unique to individual patients and team members. The uncovering of such issues requires time with the patient, in careful and respectful dialogue, exploring the meaning of the patient's refusal.

A Closing Comment

Nearly three decades ago, the President's Commission for the Study of Ethical Problems in Biomedical and Behavioral Research wisely urged "that those responsible for assessing capacity not be content with providing an answer to the question of whether or not a particular patient is incapacitated" (President's Commission, 1982, p. 173). Specifically, the Commission urged that the evaluator also pay attention to removing barriers to decisional capacity. But the point has broader implications. The capacity evaluator may often have to play an active role in resolving a problem that precipitated the initial consult request, of which the determination of capacity may only be a part. The role may involve nurturing the often fragile "autonomy" of competent patients faced with difficult decisions. It may involve helping the team and the surrogates navigate the sometimes contentious waters of surrogate decision making. And sometimes it may involve helping the team seek the formal opinion of the courts. This range of tasks within the role of the evaluator is thus quite wide, and makes the work of capacity evaluation challenging but always engaging.

Capacity to Consent to Research $\quad$ 8

C onditions such as schizophrenia and Alzheimer's disease (AD), to name just two, represent prevalent neuropsychiatric illnesses that have a devastating impact on their victims. We cannot currently alter the course of AD in truly significant ways, and schizophrenia remains a chronic, debilitating condition. The best hope for advances in treating persons with such illnesses rests on research. However, the very thing that makes these conditions so devastating—the assault on the brain that impairs the overall cognitive and decision-making abilities—creates the ethical problem of the need to conduct research with those who are often not capable of providing their own informed consent.

Research involving people who are decisionally impaired is indeed becoming much more common, and with the increasing societal focus on the ethics of research in general, the need to evaluate the consent capacity of research subjects is also increasing. For example, it is becoming more common to build capacity assessment procedures into clinical trials that involve persons who may have impaired decisional abilities (Stroup et al., 2005). The information gained from such determinations of capacity can be used in a variety of ways: the potential subject, if found incapable, may be excluded from the research, enrolled based on a surrogate's consent, or, if the subject still wishes to participate in the research, may undergo further education to see if that will improve his ability to consent.

This chapter provides an overview of how to assess research consent capacity. The overall framework is in many ways similar to the assessment of treatment consent capacity. However, the

INFO

The research context differs from the clinical context in that benefiting the subject-patient is not the primary goal of research.

research context is different from the clinical context, the most important difference being that in the clinical realm the shared assumption is the primacy of patients' interests whereas in the research context, the primary goal is the generation of scientific knowledge, whether or not the welfare of the subjects in the study is also a goal (Henderson et al., 2007). This difference leads to some necessary alterations in the capacity evaluation process.

Another difference between the contexts is that the capacity evaluator may be asked for her input not only at the stage of performing the capacity evaluations but more likely at the earlier stage of planning a study. Most research study procedures need to be approved beforehand by the local ethics review board that is variously known as the institutional review board (IRB) in the United States or as the research ethics committee (REC) or board (REB) in some other countries. And certainly any procedures that deal with how to assess the consent capacity of potentially impaired research subjects will need to be worked out well ahead of time. The discussion in this chapter is intended to aid the neuropsychiatric researcher and the capacity evaluator in working with their local research ethics review committees.

History and Legal Context

A Brief History

In the research context, the primary goal is to generate scientific knowledge; the goal of a clinical trial, for example, is not primarily to benefit those who participate in the experiment (although such benefits can occur and there is nothing wrong with hoping that such direct benefits occur; Henderson et al., 2007). This essential difference led to a much earlier recognition of the need for *informed* consent (even if it was not called informed consent at that time). For example, in 1907 Sir William Osler was asked to testify to the British Royal Commission on Vivisection regarding Major Walter Reed's experiment on yellow fever that had taken place almost a decade earlier (Jonsen, 1998). In that experiment, Reed enrolled 25 local Cubans and American soldiers in a controlled experiment, exposing some to mosquitoes who had fed on yellow fever patients and some to soiled bedding from patients (Jonsen, 1998). These volunteers signed a contract—perhaps the first informed consent document ever—that stated the purpose of the experiment and its risks and they were paid a sizable sum ($100–200 depending on whether they became ill). When Osler was asked by the Commission whether "to experiment upon man with possible ill results was immoral," he answered, "It is always immoral, without a definite, specific statement from the individual himself, with a *full knowledge of the circumstances*" (italics added, Osler quoted in Jonsen, 1998, p. 131).

The essential difference between treatment and research was formally recognized as early as 1900 in a Prussian regulation (Vollmann & Winau, 1996). And a later 1931 German regulation elaborates what is essentially a doctrine of informed consent: "Innovative therapy may be carried out only after the subject or his legal representative has unambiguously consented to the procedures in the light of relevant information provided in advance" (Sass, 1983). Thus, when the Nuremberg Code, which was enunciated by the "Nazi Doctor's Trial" court, stated that voluntary consent of the human subject is "absolutely essential" and that adequate information was necessary for "understanding and enlightened decision," it was not the first document to do so. The Nuremberg Code also elaborated the elements of disclosure for consent: "the nature, duration, and purpose of the experiment; the method and means . . . ; all inconveniences and hazards reasonable to be expected; and the effects upon his health or person" (1998). Thus, the idea that a person entering a research study needs to give not just simple consent but *informed* consent was recognized long before such a standard became common in the treatment setting. Indeed, the developments in the research consent arena no doubt shaped the informed consent doctrine in the treatment context that we have today (Manson & O'Neill, 2007).

8
chapter

Current Legal Situation

The current U.S. law of informed consent for research can be found in Title 45 of the Code of Federal Regulations, Part 46 (Department of Health and Human Services, 2005). In terms of criteria for assessing capacity, the Federal regulations are silent, although they are meticulous and comprehensive in terms of the required elements of disclosure for informed consent. Some of the new state laws that specifically address research involving incapacitated subjects do discuss the criteria for capacity. For example, the recent New Jersey statute defines "unable to consent" as

> unable to voluntarily reason, understand, and appreciate the nature and consequences of proposed health research interventions, including the subject's diagnosis and prognosis, the burdens, benefits, and risks of, and alternatives to, any such research, and to reach an informed decision. All adults are presumed to have the ability to consent unless determined otherwise pursuant to this section or other provisions of State law (New Jersey, 2008).

It further states that the evaluator will be "an attending physician with no connection to the proposed research and shall be made to a reasonable degree of medical certainty." This language should be familiar, being quite similar to the treatment consent capacity statutes. In fact, another recent law (in Virginia) simply references the definition and criteria for determining incapacity found elsewhere in the same state's statutes covering medical treatment situations (Code of Virginia). As we will see, this tendency in state laws to closely model their research ethics statutes regarding the decisionally impaired on the treatment consent context does create some need for clarification.

Conceptual Issues

In chapter 2, we discussed two main issues under this heading: one, the criteria for capacity, concentrating on the four abilities model and its relationship with other criteria as set forth in various laws, policies, and court cases; and, two, the main elements of the modern doctrine of capacity, with special focus on the function-based (rather than diagnostic) conception of capacity and the risk-sensitive application of capacity thresholds. How do these issues apply in the research context?

Criteria for Research Consent Capacity

In the research consent context the laws and regulations are even more unsettled than in the treatment consent context. If a jurisdiction does have specific statutes or regulations applicable to research involving those who are decisionally impaired, the evaluator should of course follow those requirements. However, given that even in such statutes the description of the standards for capacity will be fairly broad and in need of considerable clinical interpretation, the general principles and practices outlined in this book should be of value. If a jurisdiction does not have specific standards for research consent capacity (as in most jurisdictions), it is advisable to turn to any statutes or criteria regarding the treatment consent capacity that exist for that state, as a source of guidance.

In either situation, the four abilities model should provide a comprehensive framework to understand and organize the assessment of the essential abilities relevant for research consent. Thus, the same strategy given in chapter 2 can be applied here: use the four abilities model, as it will generally cover the criteria named in most statutes or policies. Indeed, recent national commissions such as the National Bioethics Advisory Commission (1998) explicitly used the four abilities framework in their report. The four abilities model will be a good place to start because of its conceptual and legal grounding as well as the relatively large amount of empirical data generated using the model, especially for the research context. As we will see, the relatively standardized context of the research consent situation has made it an ideal situation for research into the decision-making capacity of persons with neuropsychiatric and medical illnesses.

Elements of Disclosure for Research Informed Consent

What about the required elements of disclosure? There is a potential for conflict between state laws and Federal regulations. As we saw, a state law may elucidate some specific disclosure elements that are enumerated in its discussion of consent capacity, for example, the new New Jersey law mentions "subject's diagnosis and prognosis, the burdens, benefits, and risks of, and alternatives to, any such research," which obviously uses the same framework for disclosure for the treatment consent context. However, it leaves out some key elements such as the fact that the decision is about research and not treatment—that is, it leaves out the element of the purpose of research.

The Federal requirements for disclosure in research informed consent consist of eight items (see Table 8.1) along with six additional elements that are to be provided "when applicable" (45 CRF 46.116b).

Given the potential differences in the required elements of disclosure between a state's statute and the Federal regulations, what should the evaluator do? The theoretical answer is that the Federal requirements should take precedence—at least certain items on the Federal list should not be left out—because they are necessary to accurately characterize the nature of the decision for the patient *as a research subject*. One cannot leave out, for example, the crucial fact that what the subjects are being asked to do is participate in a research study because the primary goal of research is generation of knowledge, rather than primarily an alternative

Table 8.1	Federal Disclosure Requirements for Informed Consent for Research

(1) A statement that the study is research, its purpose and procedures
(2) Any reasonably foreseeable risks or discomforts
(3) Any benefits that may be reasonably expected
(4) Any alternative treatments that might be advantageous to the subject
(5) Degree of confidentiality expected
(6) Compensation, if any, and whether and nature of treatment available if injury occurs
(7) Contact information for further questions
(8) Statement that participation is voluntary

Source: "Protection of Human Subjects," Title 45 Code of Federal Regulations, Pt 46.116a.

treatment option for the participants. The practical answer is that a state statute's requirements when modeled solely after the treatment consent capacity context will be incomplete rather than in conflict with the Federal list, so that using the Federal guideline should also satisfy such state requirements.

But how then should the evaluator incorporate such a long list of disclosure elements into her evaluation? In practice, if the local IRB and the investigator of the research protocol have done their job, the capacity evaluator can begin with an examination of the approved informed consent form. However, even with a prepre-pared document such as the informed consent form, there will be too much *and* not enough information. It will be too much in the sense that one cannot assess every disclosure element in the testing of, say, the understanding ability. In fact, some of the elements in the Federal list are arguably more ethically important than others. A selection of the elements must be made. The job of the evaluator is to measure the *potential* for understanding, appreciation, reasoning, and so on, rather than to comprehensively assess whether, for example, the subject actually understands every single item in the informed consent form. In making a salient selection of disclosure elements, one very helpful guide is to use a tool such as the MacCAT-CR version (see discussion later in this chapter).

On the other hand, the informed consent forms may not contain enough information to guide a capacity evaluator's work. Such forms are written for a lay audience, and the capacity evaluator may need to have a deeper grasp of some of the information in order to be able to translate the often technical language into something that is more digestible, or to answer questions that are not explicitly addressed in the informed consent form, especially for those who may have some degree of impairment. This can be obtained from a conversation with the principal investigator, or reading the research protocol itself, or, ideally, both.

Risk–Benefit Calculus Is Different Than in the Treatment Context

Although the research team has the responsibility of minimizing risk to the subjects, it is not the individual subjects' welfare that is the primary goal of the research enterprise. Indeed, in most situations of research, the subject forgoes some advantage in order to enhance the goals of science (Lidz & Appelbaum, 2002). This is why there is such an elaborate system of regulatory oversight of human subject research. The implication for capacity assessment is that the threshold for competence must take into account this different risk–benefit context. This will not be an algorithm-based decision, but a clinical judgment.

Empirical Foundations and Limits

In some ways, the capacity to consent to research is better suited to empirical research than the capacity to consent to treatment because it is much easier to standardize the interview instrument as all of the subjects are facing the same decision-making situation. Thus, considerable portion of the empirical literature on consent capacity involves the research consent context. The reader is referred to chapter 3, which provides a detailed review.

Data Collection

Preparation for the Interview
CONTINUUM OF POTENTIAL PRACTICES

In most encounters between adult research subjects and researchers, the presumption of capacity is still valid. The person obtaining consent informally assesses whether the subject is able to consent, to see if there are sufficient concerns to question the presumption of capacity. Whereas in the treatment context the treatment team decides whether the presumption of capacity should be questioned, in the research context the immediate institutional authority regarding whether the subjects are likely to have impaired decisional abilities and whether a specific plan for capacity assessment is required generally rests with the local IRB. However, there are no uniform standards or even guidelines for formulating such plans. Such plans need to be flexible and adapted to the particular context. For instance, in some protocols, the capacity evaluator may be asked to evaluate a potential subject only when a certain triggering event occurs so that the evaluations are conducted on a case-by-case basis. Or, the very nature of the protocol may be such that every potential subject being evaluated for participation in the protocol will be required to undergo a formal capacity determination. Also, depending on the risk–benefit analysis of the protocol, the degree to which the procedures are prespecified and structured need to be adapted, and perhaps even a prespecified threshold for capacity may need to be described. The requirements for documentation may vary as well. There may also be variations on who may be designated as capacity evaluators, that is, whether such a person must be independent of the research team, and what type of qualifications and training are necessary in order to conduct such an assessment (Kim, Appelbaum, Jeste, & Olin, 2004; National Bioethics Advisory Commission, 1998; New Jersey, 2008).

As noted above, the capacity evaluator's expertise will likely be called upon before the IRB and the researchers finalize the procedures, because they may need assistance in setting up a procedure for a protocol. And, just as in the treatment consent context, the capacity evaluator may sometimes need to direct the interested parties away from implementing a capacity determination scheme. For example, not being sufficiently aware of the risk-sensitive standard of assessing capacity, an overzealous IRB may suggest an elaborate capacity assessment scheme for a very low-risk study. The overly conservative, risk-aversive nature of some IRBs is an increasingly discussed phenomenon (Fost & Levine, 2007). But an elaborate capacity evaluation of everyone entering a low-risk study (e.g., a benign interview study) is unnecessary and the capacity evaluator's job may sometimes be to educate the IRB.

The rigor or intensiveness of capacity evaluation will vary

INFO

Although no universally accepted standard for research consent capacity exists, its assessment should follow the general principles of assessing function (abilities relevant to capacity) in context (the risks and benefits posed by the research protocol).

8
chapter

depending on the subject population and the risks and benefit profile of the protocol. At one extreme may be an informal, impressionistic judgment of a research assistant. This may be appropriate, for example, for a minimal risk study involving AD patients, with no sensitive information, or for studies that have been deemed exempt from IRB review. At the other extreme for capacity evaluation procedures may be a systematic, structured evaluation by an experienced, independent mental health professional who renders his judgment using a detailed and validated capacity assessment tool. Perhaps this may be an appropriate standard when enrolling potentially impaired persons who provide their own informed consent for a high-risk study, such as first in human neurosurgical experiments.

But what about those cases that fall somewhere in between? There are currently no widely accepted standards or practices. There is a great deal of interest in developing brief forms or questionnaires for use in documenting the fact that subjects have understood the essential elements of informed consent, or for use as an initial screen to determine whether further, more intensive assessment is needed (Palmer et al., 2005).

CAPACITY EVALUATOR'S UNDERSTANDING OF THE RESEARCH PROTOCOL

Just as the evaluator in the clinical context has the responsibility of understanding what is being asked of the patient (the nature of the patient's condition, the proposed alternatives and their likely consequences, etc.), the evaluator in the research consent context must familiarize herself with the research protocol and especially what the subjects are being told. Because most mental health professionals who conduct capacity evaluations are not researchers, and given that each research protocol has its own purpose, procedures, risks, and potential benefits, the capacity evaluator will need to do some homework.

In this regard, as noted above, much of the hard work will have been done for the evaluator because the researchers and the IRB will have agreed upon a written document enumerating all the legally required elements of informed consent. The regulations in fact require that the form be written and conveyed in such a way that the language is "understandable" (45 CFR 46.116). The capacity evaluator must thoroughly familiarize himself with the elements contained in the informed consent form. Ideally, the evaluator should discuss directly with the principal investigator at the outset of the research project regarding the purpose, design, and other elements of the protocol.

The evaluator should have a clear idea of the risks and burdens to the subjects as well as any loss in individualized care or other loss of usually expected benefits that a subject-patient otherwise would receive if not in a research study. There are many questions that could be asked. Regarding the protocol, the capacity evaluator should explore:

- What is the purpose of the study?
- Is the research procedure designed to gain scientific knowledge only (i.e., a study of pathophysiological process), rather than an experiment to test a potential treatment (or a combination)?
- Is the study a first in human experiment that is primarily designed to see how the intervention is tolerated, with no reasonable expectation of benefit to the subjects?
- Or is it a study designed to confirm the efficacy of an intervention that has already shown some promise in previous controlled studies?
- Is the placebo arm a benign intervention (such as a sugar pill) or is it an active simulation placebo (such as sham surgery)?
- If a placebo control is to be used, are there alternative efficacious treatments for the subject's condition, or is the subject's condition that has no known effective treatments?
- If a placebo is to be used when effective treatments exist, do many patients forgo treatment or discontinue treatment because of common, intolerable side effects, such that those selected for the study may not be forgoing a good at all?

There are also important questions about the study sample as well:

- Are these subjects who have already failed a series of treatments such that for them there are no other known efficacious alternatives to treatment?
- Or can they be treated with other therapies, and their participation consists of forgoing a potential good that they otherwise could expect outside the research context?

Overall, the key question is, What are the potentially negative consequences for the subject, whether in terms of risks or due to forgoing of otherwise entitled or available benefit, from being in the research study?

Advisability of Using Structured Instruments

There are several good reasons why, in the research consent context, the capacity evaluator should opt for a standard instrument to guide her evaluation. First, by its very nature, a research protocol is standardized in its selection of subjects and in its procedures. Thus, the research consent situation presents the same decision-making scenario to each potential subject and it naturally lends itself to a standardized approach. Second, as noted above, the informed consent forms are often much too long to be used effectively as a guide to assessment; a judicious selection of elements must be made, and using a standardized form that has been well validated will make the job of the evaluator much easier. Third, there is now considerable data showing that research assistant level personnel can administer and score these instruments reliably (Kim et al., 2001; Kim et al., 2007). This may allow a more efficient two-step process in which the capacity evaluator can use the initial screening data (obtained by an assistant) from a standardized instrument to engage in a more focused interview. Fourth, for certain groups of patients, it may be possible to use published research data using the same instruments to help guide the evaluation process, perhaps even by establishing benchmarks for thresholds of capacity for studies with similar levels of risk (Karlawish et al., 2008; Kim et al., 2007).

For the above reasons, anyone either advising a research team in formulating a capacity evaluation plan or carrying out the plan itself should use a structured approach that has some empirical data behind it. Of course, which instrument to use may depend on the situation. The greater the need to ensure a thorough and well-documented assessment, the stronger the reason to use, for example, an instrument such as the MacCAT-CR (Appelbaum & Grisso, 2001), which has been validated for use in a variety of research subject populations. However, if the risks are lower and a less intensive or formal examination is needed, then beginning with a briefer screening instrument may be appropriate in some situations (Palmer et al., 2005).

One important option should not be overlooked. For certain populations, there is ample data showing that understanding improves with interventions, for example, persons with schizophrenia who are eligible for research studies (Carpenter et al., 2000; Dunn et al., 2001; Moser et al., 2005; Wirshing et al., 1998). Because most of these studies show that a variety of measures can improve the understanding of most of the subjects, perhaps the resources should be spent on optimizing informed consent procedures as well as on measuring decisional abilities.

Interpretation

Considerations in Setting the Capacity Threshold

Because the research context has a different risk–benefit situation than the clinical context, it is important for the evaluator to set the threshold properly, taking into account several issues. First, not only risks but the loss of otherwise available benefits should be taken into account. Any restrictions on the treatment changes during a clinical trial, in order to maintain standard conditions, will mean that the subject agrees to a practice that is in general not designed to maximize his well-being but to maximize the validity and reliability of the data. Second, the relevant benefits to be counted in the risk–benefit calculus are direct benefits to the subject, not the benefits of research for society and science. The latter should not count in the overall risk–benefit calculus in

BEWARE
The research benefits to society and to science should not weigh in the overall risk–benefit calculus of the capacity evaluation in the research context.

the determination of the subject's capacity because to do so would be to build in an interest of society in the evaluation when it should not be a consideration. Third, although in the treatment consent situation the risk–benefit calculus may be different depending on the choice that the patient makes (e.g., accepting a high-benefit, low-risk treatment versus refusing such a treatment), this issue is moot in the research context because the only question of interest is whether or not the person has the capacity to consent to participation. If the patient refuses, then that is the end of the matter, and further questions of capacity need not be pursued.

Maintaining an Independent Point of View

Because the primary aim of clinical research is to generate scientific knowledge and not the individualized treatment for the research subject, a researcher (or a team member) who conducts the capacity evaluation herself faces a conflict of interest. On the one hand, there is an incentive to include as many eligible subjects into the protocol as efficiently as possible. On the other, the capacity judgment should be based on balancing the autonomy–welfare considerations for the subject. This is why the need for an independent evaluation increases as the risk–benefit ratio becomes less favorable to the subjects. A minimal risk interview study involving persons with AD, for example, may require only informal evaluation of the subject's capacity by the researcher to assess whether the person is capable of consenting to the study. But for a first in human neuro-surgical experiment involving gene transfer for a dementing illness, the need for an independent opinion is high and the threshold for capacity would be correspondingly high as well.

How Long Must the Patient Retain Information?

Sometimes a question is raised as to how long should a patient retain the information in order to be considered competent. As noted in chapter 5, obviously, retention of information is necessary for at least a short term, at least for as long as the period relevant for decision making. But beyond this, there is no universally accepted answer.

A slightly different but commonly asked question is: What happens if the subject loses her consent capacity during the course of the research study? Generally, these cases can be divided into two categories. One, it may be predictable that the person will lose capacity during the course of the research (suppose, e.g., the person's initial mild dementia deteriorates predictably, or it is known that the condition involves fluctuations in symptoms that affect decisional abilities), in which case the eventuality of such situations should be discussed as part of the initial informed consent process. As long as there are no significant new developments, such as changes in the protocol, in its risks and benefits, and in the participant's clinical state, then some argue that there is no need for a reconsent (Wendler & Rackoff, 2002) and by implication there would be no need for a reassessment of capacity. Two, the loss of capacity may be unanticipated or changes may occur in the study that require a reassurance that the subject is still providing informed consent (e.g., if data show a signal during a clinical trial that may not justify halting the trial but certainly would require informing the participants, the natural question arises as to whether the participants at that point are competent to use that new information).

It should be noted, however, that the ethics of this issue are quite unsettled, with some arguing that there is a reason to assess and document that subjects are maintaining their informed consent regardless of whether there are triggering events during the course of a research study. One such interdisciplinary working group composed of experts in schizophrenia research, bioethics, and law, for example, has proposed that the following questions (Assessment of Sustained Informed Consent Questions; Prentice, Appelbaum, Conley, & Carpenter, 2007) be used as an interim screen to assure that a reasonable degree of informed consent is maintained:

- Are you participating in a research study?
- What is the general purpose of the study?

- Are you required to participate in this research study?
- Is the treatment you are getting now the same as it was before you started the study?
- Are you allowed to withdraw from the study?
- If you decide to withdraw, will you be able to receive treatment?
- Are there any possible risks or discomforts in the study?

Again, there are no established policies on how to handle fluctuations in decisional capacity during the course of a lengthy protocol. Until such policies are established, a reasonable course is to anticipate whether and how the subjects in a protocol may lose decisional capacity, and think through in advance whether the informed consent process should explicitly addresses any anticipated loss of capacity and whether unexpected losses need to be monitored (versus only when certain triggering events occur).

After the Assessment

There are several issues that still need to be considered after a potential subject's research consent capacity has been determined. If the person has been determined to lack the capacity to provide informed consent, there are three options: the person can be excluded from enrolling; the person can be given an opportunity to improve his performance, if the subject still desires to participate in the research; and finally, a surrogate may provide permission. When an incompetent person refuses to participate in research, the person should not be enrolled. The occasional dilemma one faces in the treatment context of an incompetent patient who refuses a highly beneficial treatment does not generally occur in research, because even the most promising experimental treatment cannot be said to have established efficacy and safety.

Remediation

Remediation of impaired subjects is an important option (Dunn & Jeste, 2001). Indeed, as indicated above, at least for persons with chronic psychoses, the evidence for interventions improving understanding is very strong. In fact, the evidence is strong enough that it might even make sense to devote most of the resources into improving informed consent whenever this population is solicited for research, rather than spending a lot of energy and resources assessing and documenting impairment. In other words, in most situations involving persons with chronic psychoses who are outpatients, the evidence is fairly clear that education and reinforcement of information will significantly enhance their understanding to the point of comparability with normal controls (Carpenter et al., 2000; Dunn et al., 2001; Palmer et al., 2004). Given this, it makes sense to devote resources to the improvement of the informed consent of such persons rather than to the measurement of their capacity. Of course, as the risk of the research increases, it may be necessary to do both, to provide an improved consent process and to assess and document the subjects' consent capacity.

As discussed in chapter 3, most methods of remediation seem to enhance understanding. These include computer-assisted slide presentations (Dunn et al., 2001), use of DVD presentation describing the research, and other less technical means (Carpenter et al., 2000; Moser et al., 2005; Wirshing et al., 1998).

Surrogate Consent for Research

If the potential subject remains incapacitated—a likely scenario when the condition involves the learning ability itself, such as AD—then the issue of enrolling subjects with surrogate permission is raised. Although the need for informed consent in research has long been recognized, how best to regulate research involving those who cannot consent for themselves has remained controversial and unsettled in policy (Kim et al., 2004; Wendler & Prasad, 2001). This issue applies not only to psychiatric and neurological research but also to research involving persons who are severely medically ill, as happens in research protocols in intensive care units (Ciroldi et al., 2007; Silverman, Luce, & Schwartz, 2004).

8
chapter

BEWARE
Many states lack laws addressing surrogate consent for research and even when they exist, they are not uniform and are often unclear.

As of this writing, the legal policy remains largely unresolved in the United States. Specifically, the Federal research regulations require that for an incompetent adult, a legally authorized representative (LAR) provide permission for the incapacitated subject to participate in research (45 CFR 46.102c). However, the regulations defer to the states on who can serve as LAR and most states have not addressed the issue clearly, if at all (Saks, Dunn, Wimer, Gonzales, & Kim, 2008). Further, there is controversy over which additional protections may be needed when incapacitated subjects are enrolled in research (Kim et al., 2004). For example, the recent law passed in California does not limit the research by specifying risk–benefit categories, leaving the judgment to local research ethics review boards, whereas laws in Virginia and New Jersey do spell out the types of research allowed in terms of risks and benefits (California, 2002; Code of Virginia, 2002; New Jersey, 2008). The capacity evaluator who becomes involved in research consent capacity evaluations should familiarize herself with the current situation in her own jurisdiction, although in most states, things remain quite murky.

What happens in states with unclear or no laws regarding surrogate consent for research? It is likely that the researcher's institution will have developed either a practice or even a written policy, taking into account the unclear legal situation. Such practices may vary among institutions within the same state, simply because they may have a variety of legal interpretations and risk management strategies (or, perhaps, no strategies at all). Indeed, in some states, such as New York, there may be different rules for researchers according to which state agency is deemed to have jurisdiction over the research study.

Surrogate Decision Making: Some Considerations

Although there is a tendency to see surrogate decision making as a uniform practice, in fact the specific context—the clinical state of the subject-patient as well as some sociocultural issues—is important in determining how such decisions are made.

DEMENTIA RESEARCH

Consider first the context of dementia research. When a person has been deemed incapable of providing informed consent for research, it means that he lacks sufficient abilities to provide *independent* informed consent. However, this does not mean that the person with dementia lacks other ethically relevant abilities such as the ability to convey a preference, the ability to work cooperatively with a loved one, or the ability to delegate her authority to a trusted surrogate (Kim & Appelbaum, 2006). Consider for instance one of the discredited criteria for competence: whether or not a person's choice is "reasonable" (e.g., whether the choice is what most people in a similar situation would make). Although this criterion is rightly rejected as a criterion for capacity, empirical data on how subjects perform on such a criterion is actually quite informative. In studies of persons with AD, it has been repeatedly shown that despite the obvious and significant loss in the ability to provide independent informed consent, such persons still tend to make choices that are similar to age-matched controls and choices that are, in the main, quite reasonable (Kim et al., 2002a; Marson et al., 1995b).

Thus, although from a legal point of view a definite final authority for decisions may be necessary, there is an important ethical reason to include the subject-patient in the decision-making process as much as is feasible in dementia research. Such patients retain veto power, for example. But more importantly, the research team should be advised to work together with the surrogate and the subject-patient, rather than treat the incompetent subject as someone who cannot contribute to the decision-making process at all. The construct of decisional competence primarily serves the purpose of attributing final decisional authority, but it fails to capture some important ethical abilities that may still be retained by the subject-patient.

Another important aspect of surrogate decision making for dementia research participants is that the surrogates tend to be involved family members (spouse or adult child) who would

8
chapter

typically be available and are relied upon to make decisions for the patient in the medical context. Thus, the reliability and availability of surrogates can be counted on in most dementia research contexts.

CRITICAL CARE RESEARCH

In contrast, research with severely ill ICU patients involves a different context. The subject-patients in such situations are not even able to assent, because quite often they are sedated or unconscious. Thus, unlike the dementia research context in which the subjects do have some remaining, ethically relevant preferences and abilities, the critical care research context poses an almost entirely unilateral substituted decision making by the surrogates. This is why ethics research in this area has tended to focus on the concordance between what the patients would have wanted and what the surrogates believe the surrogates would want, with discordance rates ranging from 20 to 42% depending on the type of hypothetical decisions posed (Ciroldi et al., 2007; Coppolino & Ackerson, 2001).

CHRONIC PSYCHOSES RESEARCH

Research involving persons with chronic psychoses (schizophrenia and schizoaffective disorders) is yet another context in which persons with impaired decisional abilities are enrolled. In contrast to dementia research or ICU research, generally such patients can be enrolled in research with their own consent (Kim et al., 2007; Stroup et al., 2005). Thus, true surrogate consent for research involving such patients generally does not arise in most research contexts although it is a theoretical possibility. Further, the additional legal restrictions on the administration of psychotropic medications to incapacitated persons in many jurisdictions adds another complication and makes it less likely that surrogate consent will be used for this population. Finally, the social context for these patients is also quite different from, for instance, patients with dementias. Persons with chronic psychoses tend to be more socially disconnected. When research studies have attempted to provide "subject advocates" for such subjects, most subjects did not have close family members available to serve this role (Stroup & Appelbaum, 2003).

Summary

Serious brain disorders are some of the most common and devastating public health problems we face today. Research into such disorders, however, will involve persons who may have difficulty providing their own informed consent. As research protocols become more innovative, they may also involve novel and unknown risks, and the need to prospectively (and perhaps periodically) assess the subjects' capacity will increase. Although the risk–benefit considerations are qualitatively different from the treatment consent context, the basic principles (e.g., importance of the risk–benefit profile) and the framework (four abilities relevant to capacity) still provide guidance for the evaluator. The challenge for the evaluator will be the application of these familiar principles in a new context. Hopefully, as the practice of research consent capacity assessment becomes more common, more widely accepted standards of application will be developed to aid such assessments.

References

Adamis, D., Martin, F. C., Treloar, A., & Macdonald, A. J. (2005). Capacity, consent, and selection bias in a study of delirium. *Journal of Medical Ethics, 31*, 137–143.

American Bar Association. (2008a). *Health care power of attorney and combined advance directive legislation—January 2008*. Washington, DC: American Bar Association.

American Bar Association. (2008b). *Surrogate consent in the absence of an advance directive—January 2008*. Washington, DC: American Bar Association.

American Psychiatric Association. (1994). *Diagnostic and statistical manual of mental disorders* (4th ed.). Washington, DC: American Psychiatric Association.

Appelbaum, B. C., Appelbaum, P. S., & Grisso, T. (1998). Competence to consent to voluntary psychiatric hospitalization: A test of a standard proposed by APA. American Psychiatric Association. *Psychiatric Services, 49*, 1193–1196.

Appelbaum, P. S. (1994). *Almost a revolution*. New York: Oxford University Press.

Appelbaum, P. S. (2004). Law & psychiatry: Psychiatric advance directives and the treatment of committed patients. *Psychiatric Services, 55*, 751–763.

Appelbaum, P. S. (2007). Assessment of patients' competence to consent to treatment. *New England Journal of Medicine, 357*, 1834–1840.

Appelbaum, P. S., & Grisso, T. (1988). Assessing patients' capacities to consent to treatment. *New England Journal of Medicine, 319*, 1635–1638.

Appelbaum, P. S., & Grisso, T. (1995). The MacArthur Treatment Competence Study. I: Mental illness and competence to consent to treatment. *Law and Human Behavior, 19*, 105–126.

Appelbaum, P. S., & Grisso, T. (1997). Capacities of hospitalized, medically ill patients to consent to treatment. *Psychosomatics, 38*, 119–125.

Appelbaum, P. S., & Grisso, T. (2001). *MacCAT-CR: MacArthur competence assessment tool for clinical research*. Sarasota, FL: Professional Resource Press.

Appelbaum, P. S., Grisso, T., Frank, E., O'Donnell, S., & Kupfer, D. (1999). Competence of depressed patients for consent to research. *American Journal of Psychiatry, 156*, 1380–1384.

Appelbaum, P. S., & Roth, L. H. (1982). Competency to consent to research: A psychiatric overview. *Archives of General Psychiatry, 39,* 951–958.

Auerswald, K. B., Charpentier, P. A., & Inouye, S. K. (1997). The informed consent process in older patients who developed delirium: A clinical epidemiologic study. *American Journal of Medicine, 103,* 410–418.

Barton, C. D. J., Mallik, H. S., Orr, W. B., & Janofsky, J. S. (1996). Clinicians' judgement of capacity of nursing home patients to give informed consent. *Psychiatric Services, 47,* 956–960.

Bassett, S. S. (1999). Attention: Neuropsychological predictor of competency in Alzheimer's disease. *Journal of Geriatric Psychiatry and Neurology, 12,* 200–205.

Bean, G., Nishisato, S., Rector, N. A., & Glancy, G. (1994). The psychometric properties of the Competency Interview Schedule. *Canadian Journal of Psychiatry. Revue Canadienne de Psychiatrie, 39,* 368–376.

Bechtold, K. T., Horner, M. D., Labbate, L. A., & Windham, W. K. (2001). The construct validity and clinical utility of the Frank Jones story as a brief screening measure of cognitive dysfunction. *Psychosomatics, 42,* 146–149.

Beckett, J., & Chaplin, R. (2006). Capacity to consent to treatment in patients with acute mania. *Psychiatric Bulletin, 30,* 419–422.

Benson, P., Roth, L. H., Appelbaum, P. S., Lidz, C., & Winslade, W. (1988). Information disclosure, subject understanding, and informed consent in psychiatric research. *Law and Human Behavior, 12,* 455–475.

Berg, J. W., Appelbaum, P. S., & Grisso, T. (1996). Constructing competence: Formulating standards of legal competence to make medical decisions. *Rutgers Law Review, 48,* 345–396.

Berg, J. W., Appelbaum, P. S., Lidz, C. W., & Parker, L. S. (2001). *Informed consent: Legal theory and clinical practice* (2nd ed.). New York: Oxford University Press.

Bourgeois, M. S. (1993). Effects of memory aids on the dyadic conversations of individuals with dementia. *Journal of Applied Behavior Analysis, 26,* 77–87.

Buchanan, A. E., & Brock, D. W. (1989). *Deciding for others: The ethics of surrogate decision making.* New York: Cambridge University Press.

Buckles, V., Powlishta, K., Palmer, J., Coats, M., Hosto, T., Buckely, A. et al. (2003). Understanding of informed consent by demented individuals. *Neurology, 62,* 1662–1666.

Carney, M., Neugroschl, R., Morrison, R., Marin, D., & Siu, A. (2001). The development and piloting of a capacity assessment tool. *Journal of Clinical Ethics, 12,* 17–22.

Carpenter, W. T., Jr., Gold, J., Lahti, A., Queern, C., Conley, R., Bartko, J., et al. (2000). Decisional capacity for informed consent in schizophrenia research. *Archives of General Psychiatry, 57,* 533–538.

Casarett, D. J., Karlawish, J. H. T., & Hirschman, K. B. (2003). Identifying ambulatory cancer patients at risk of impaired capacity to consent to research. *Journal of Pain and Symptom Management, 26*, 615–624.

Cassem, N., & Murray, G. (1997). Delirious patients. In N. Cassem, T. Stern, J. Rosenbaum, & M. Jellinek (Eds.), *Massachusetts general hospital handbook of general hospital psychiatry* (4th ed., pp. 101–122). St. Louis, MO: Mosby.

Cea, C. D., & Fisher, C. B. (2003). Health care decision-making by adults with mental retardation. *Mental Retardation, 41*, 78–87.

Charland, L. (2002). Cynthia's dilemma: Consenting to heroin prescription. *American Journal of Bioethics, 2*, 37–47.

Christensen, K., Haroun, A., Schneiderman, L. J., & Jeste, D. V. (1995). Decision-making capacity for informed consent in the older population. *Bulletin of the American Academy of Psychiatry and the Law, 23*, 353–365.

Ciroldi, M., Cariou, A., Adrie, C., Annane, D., Castelain, V., Cohen, Y., et al. (2007). Ability of family members to predict patient's consent to critical care research. *Intensive Care Medicine, 33*, 807–813.

Cohen, L. M., Dobscha, S. K., Hails, K. C., Pekow, P. S., & Chochinov, H. M. (2002). Depression and suicidal ideation in patients who discontinue the life-support treatment of dialysis. *Psychosomatic Medicine, 64*, 889–896.

Cohen, L. M., McCue, J. D., & Green, G. M. (1993). Do clinical and formal assessments of the capacity of patients in the intensive care unit to make decisions agree? *Archives of Internal Medicine, 153*, 2481–2485.

Cohen, P. (2002). Untreated addiction imposes an ethical bar to recruiting addicts for non-therapeutic studies of addictive drugs. *Journal of Law, Medicine and Ethics, 30*, 73–81.

Committee on Bioethics. (1999). Sterilization of minors with developmental disabilities. *Pediatrics, 104*, 337–340.

Coppolino, M., & Ackerson, L. (2001). Do surrogate decision makers provide accurate consent for intensive care research? *Chest, 119*, 603–612.

Cranston, R., Marson, D., Dymek, M., & Karlawish, J. (2001). Competency to consent to medical treatment in cognitively impaired patients with Parkinson's disease. *Neurology, 56*, 1782–1783.

Dellasega, C., Frank, L., & Smyer, M. (1996). Medical decision-making capacity in elderly hospitalized patients. *Journal of Ethics Law and Aging, 2*, 65–74.

Department for Constitutional Affairs. (2007). *Mental Capacity Act 2005 Code of Practice.* Retrieved July 31, 2009, from http://www.dca.gov.uk/legal-policy/mental-capacity/mca-cp.pdf

Department of Health and Human Services. (2005). *Code of Federal Regulations Title 45: Public Welfare, Part 46: Protection of Human Subjects.*

DeRenzo, E. G., Conley, R. R., & Love, R. (1998). Assessment of capacity to give consent to research participation: State of the art and beyond. *Journal of Health Care Law and Policy, 1*, 66–87.

Drane, J. F. (1984). Competency to give an informed consent. A model for making clinical assessments. *Journal of American Medical Association, 252*, 925–927.

Draper, R. J., & Dawson, D. (1990). Competence to consent to treatment: A guide for the psychiatrist. *Canadian Journal of Psychiatry. Revue Canadienne de Psychiatrie, 35*, 285–289.

Dubler, N., & White, A. (1995). Fertility control: Legal and regulatory issues. In W. T. Reich (Ed.), *Encyclopedia of bioethics* (pp. 839–847). New York: Simon and Shuster Macmillan.

Dunn, L., & Jeste, D. V. (2001). Enhancing informed consent: A review. *Neuropsychopharmacology, 24*, 595–607.

Dunn, L. B., Lindamer, L. A., Palmer, B. W., Golshan, S., Schneiderman, L., & Jeste, D. V. (2002). Improving understanding of research consent in middle-aged and elderly patients with psychotic disorders. *American Journal of Geriatric Psychiatry, 10*, 142–150.

Dunn, L. B., Lindamer, L. A., Palmer, B. W., Schneiderman, L. J., & Jeste, D. V. (2001). Enhancing comprehension of consent for research in older patients with psychosis: A randomized study of a novel consent procedure. *American Journal of Psychiatry, 158*, 1911–1913.

Dunn, L. B., Nowrangi, M. A., Palmer, B. W., Jeste, D. V., & Saks, E. R. (2006). Assessing decisional capacity for clinical research or treatment: A review of instruments. *American Journal of Psychiatry, 163*, 1323–1334.

Dymek, M., Atchison, P., Harrell, L., & Marson, D. C. (2001). Competency to consent to medical treatment in cognitively impaired patients with Parkinson's disease. *Neurology, 56*, 17–24.

Dymek, M., Marson, D., & Harrell, L. (1999). Factor structure of capacity to consent to medical treatment in patients with Alzheimer's disease: An exploratory study. *Journal of Forensic Neuropsychology, 1*, 27–48.

Earnst, K., Marson, D. C., & Harrell, L. E. (2000). Cognitive models of physicians' legal standard and personal judgments of competency in patients with Alzheimer's disease. *Journal of the American Geriatrics Society, 48*, 919–927.

Edelstein, B. (1999). *Hopemont capacity assessment interview manual and scoring guide*. Morgantown, WV: West Virginia University.

Elbogen, E. B., Swanson, J. W., Appelbaum, P. S., Swartz, M. S., Ferron, J., Van Dorn, R. A., et al. (2007). Competence to complete psychiatric advance directives: Effects of facilitated decision making. *Law and Human Behavior, 31*, 275–289.

Elias, W. J., & Cosgrove, G. R. (2008). Psychosurgery. *Neurosurgical Focus, 25*, E1.

Elliott, C. (1997). Caring about risks. Are severely depressed patients competent to consent to research? *Archives of General Psychiatry, 54*, 113–116.

Emanuel, L. L., Emanuel, E. J., Stoeckle, J. D., Hummel, L. R., & Barry, M. J. (1994). Advance directives—Stability of patients treatment choices. *Archives of Internal Medicine, 154*, 209–217.

Etchells, E., Darzins, P., Silberfeld, M., Singer, P. A., McKenny, J., Naglie, G., et al. (1999). Assessment of patient capacity to consent to treatment. *Journal of General Internal Medicine, 14*, 27–34.

Faden, R., & Beauchamp, T. (1986). *A history and theory of informed consent.* New York: Oxford University Press.

Fagerlin, A., & Schneider, C. E. (2004). Enough: The failure of the living will. *Hastings Center Report, 34*, 30–42.

Farnsworth, M. G. (1990). Competency evaluations in a general hospital. *Psychosomatics, 31*, 60–66.

Fazel, S., Hope, T., & Jacoby, R. (1999). Assessment of competence to complete advance directives: Validation of a patient centred approach. *British Medical Journal, 318*, 493–497.

Ferrand, E., Bachoud-Levi, A. C., Rodrigues, M., Maggiore, S., Brun-Buisson, C., & Lemaire, F. (2001). Decision-making capacity and surrogate designation in French ICU patients. *Intensive Care Medicine, 27*, 1360–1364.

Fisher, C. B., Cea, C. D., Davidson, P. W., & Fried, A. L. (2006). Capacity of persons with mental retardation to consent to participate in randomized clinical trials. *American Journal of Psychiatry, 163*, 1813–1820.

Fitten, L. J., Lusky, R., & Hamann, C. (1990). Assessing treatment decision-making capacity in elderly nursing home residents. *Journal of the American Geriatrics Society, 38*, 1097–1104.

Fitten, L. J., & Waite, M. S. (1990). Impact of medical hospitalization on treatment decision-making capacity in the elderly. *Archives of Internal Medicine, 150*, 1717–1721.

Folstein, M. F., Folstein, S. E., & McHugh, P. (1975). Mini-Mental State. A practical guide for grading the cognitive state of patients for the clinician. *Journal of Psychiatric Research, 12*, 189–198.

Fost, N., & Levine, R. J. (2007). The dysregulation of human subjects research. *JAMA: The Journal of the American Medical Association, 298*, 2196–2198.

Ganzini, L., Lee, M. A., Heintz, R. T., Bloom, J. D., & Fenn, D. S. (1994). The effect of depression treatment on elderly patients' preferences for life-sustaining medical therapy. *American Journal of Psychiatry, 151*, 1631–1636.

Ganzini, L., Volicer, L., Nelson, W., & Derse, A. (2003). Pitfalls in assessment of decision-making capacity. *Psychosomatics, 44*, 237–243.

Garrison, M., & Schneider, C. E. (2003). *The law of bioethics: Individual autonomy and social regulation.* St. Paul, MN: West Group.

Goodwin, P. E., Smyer, M. A., & Lair, T. I. (1995). Decision-making incapacity among nursing home residents: Results from the 1987 NMES survey. *Behavioral Sciences and the Law, 13,* 405–414.

Grisso, T. (2003). *Evaluating competencies* (2nd ed.). New York: Kluwer/Plenum.

Grisso, T., & Appelbaum, P. S. (1995). The MacArthur Treatment Competence Study. III: Abilities of patients to consent to psychiatric and medical treatments. *Law and Human Behavior, 19,* 149–174.

Grisso, T., & Appelbaum, P. S. (1998). *Assessing competence to consent to treatment: A guide for physicians and other health professionals.* New York: Oxford University Press.

Grisso, T., & Appelbaum, P. S. (2006). Appreciating anorexia: Decisional capacity and the role of values. *Philosophy, Psychiatry, Psychology, 13,* 293–297.

Grisso, T., Appelbaum, P. S., & Hill-Fotouhi, C. (1997). The MacCAT-T: A clinical tool to assess patients' capacities to make treatment decisions. *Psychiatric Services, 48,* 1415–1419.

Grisso, T., Appelbaum, P. S., Mulvey, E. P., & Fletcher, K. (1995). The MacArthur Treatment Competence Study. II: Measures of abilities related to competence to consent to treatment. *Law and Human Behavior, 19,* 127–148.

Grossman, L., & Summers, F. (1980). A study of the capacity of schizophrenic patients to give informed consent. *Hospital and Community Psychiatry, 31,* 205–206.

Groves, J. E. (1978). Taking care of the hateful patient. *New England Journal of Medicine, 298,* 883–887.

von Gunten, A., Ostos-Wiechetek, M., Brull, J., Vaudaux-Pisquem, I., Cattin, S., & Duc, R. (2008). Clock-drawing test performance in the normal elderly and its dependence on age and education. *European Neurology, 60,* 73–78.

Gutheil, T. G., & Appelbaum, P. S. (2000). *Clinical handbook of psychiatry and the law* (3rd ed.). Philadelphia, PA: Lippincott Williams and Wilkins.

Gutheil, T. G., & Bursztajn, H. J. (1986). Clinicians' guidelines for assessing and presenting subtle forms of patient incompetence in legal settings. *The American Journal of Psychiatry, 143,* 1020–1023.

Hazelton, L. D., Sterns, G. L., & Chisholm, T. (2003). Decision-making capacity and alcohol abuse: Clinical and ethical considerations in personal care choices. *General Hospital Psychiatry, 25,* 130–135.

Henderson, C., Swanson, J. W., Szmukler, G., Thornicroft, G., & Zinkler, M. (2008). A typology of advance statements in mental health care. *Psychiatric Services, 59,* 63–71.

Henderson, G. E., Churchill, L. R., Davis, A. M., Easter, M. M., Grady, C., Joffe, S., et al. (2007). Clinical trials and medical care: Defining the therapeutic misconception. *PLoS Medicine, 4,* e324.

Holzer, J. C., Gansler, D. A., Moczynski, N. P., & Folstein, M. F. (1997). Cognitive functions in the informed consent evaluation process: A pilot study. *Journal of the American Academy of Psychiatry and the Law, 25,* 531–540.

Hurst, S. A. (2004). When patients refuse assessment of decision-making capacity: How should clinicians respond? *Archives of Internal Medicine, 164*(16), 1757–1760.

Inouye, S. K. (2006). Delirium in older persons. *New England Journal of Medicine, 354,* 1157–1165.

Irwin, M., Lovitz, A., Marder, S. R., Mintz, J., Winslade, W., Van Putten, T., et al. (1985). Psychotic patients' understanding of informed consent. *American Journal of Psychiatry, 142,* 1351–1354.

Janofsky, J. S., McCarthy, R. J., & Folstein, M. F. (1992). The Hopkins Competency Assessment Test: A brief method for evaluating patients' capacity to give informed consent. *Hospital and Community Psychiatry, 43,* 132–136.

Jonsen, A. R. (1998). *The birth of bioethics.* New York: Oxford University Press.

Jonsen, A. R., Siegler, M., & Winslade, W. (1998). *Clinical ethics.* New York: McGraw-Hill.

Jourdan, J. B., & Glickman, L. (1991). Reasons for requests for evaluation of competency in a municipal general hospital. *Psychosomatics, 32,* 413–416.

Juster, F., & Suzman, R. (1995). An overview of the Health and Retirement Study. *The Journal of Human Resources, 30,* S7–S56.

Karlawish, J. H. T., Casarett, D. J., James, B. D., Xie, S. X., & Kim, S. Y. H. (2005). The ability of persons with Alzheimer disease (AD) to make a decision about taking an AD treatment. *Neurology, 64,* 1514–1519.

Karlawish, J. H. T., Kim, S. Y. H., Knopman, D., van Dyck, C. H., James, B. D., & Marson, D. (2008). Interpreting the clinical significance of capacity scores for informed consent in Alzheimer disease clinical trials. *American Journal of Geriatric Psychiatry, 16,* 568–574.

Karlawish, J. H. T., Knopman, D., Clark, C. M., Morris, J. C., Marson, D., Whitehouse, P. J., et al. (2002). Informed consent for Alzheimer's disease clinical trials: A survey of clinical investigators. *IRB: Ethics and Human Research, 24,* 1–5.

Katz, M., Abbey, S., Rydall, A., & Lowy, F. (1995). Psychiatric consultation for competency to refuse medical treatment. A retrospective study of patient characteristics and outcome. *Psychosomatics, 36,* 33–41.

Kim, S. Y., & Cist, A. F. (2004). Treatment decisions at the end of life. In T. Stern, J. Herman, & P. Slavin (Eds.). *The MGH guide to primary care psychiatry* (pp. 687–695). New York: McGraw-Hill.

Kim, S. Y. H. (2006). When does decisional impairment become decisional incompetence? Ethical and methodological issues in capacity research in schizophrenia. *Schizophrenia Bulletin, 32,* 92–97.

Kim, S. Y. H., & Appelbaum, P. S. (2006). The capacity to appoint a proxy and the possibility of concurrent proxy directives. *Behavioral Sciences and the Law, 24,* 469–478.

Kim, S. Y. H., Appelbaum, P. S., Jeste, D. V., & Olin, J. T. (2004). Proxy and surrogate consent in geriatric neuropsychiatric research: Update and recommendations. *American Journal of Psychiatry, 161,* 797–806.

Kim, S. Y. H., Appelbaum, P. S., Swan, J., Stroup, T. S., McEvoy, J. P., Goff, D. C., et al. (2007). Determining when impairment constitutes incapacity for informed consent in schizophrenia research. *The British Journal of Psychiatry, 191,* 38–43.

Kim, S. Y. H., & Caine, E. D. (2002). Utility and limits of the mini mental state examination in evaluating consent capacity in Alzheimer's disease. *Psychiatric Services, 53,* 1322–1324.

Kim, S. Y. H., Caine, E. D., Currier, G. W., Leibovici, A., & Ryan, J. M. (2001). Assessing the competence of persons with Alzheimer's disease in providing informed consent for participation in research. *American Journal of Psychiatry, 158,* 712–717.

Kim, S. Y. H., Caine, E. D., Swan, J., & Appelbaum, P. S. (2006). Do clinicians follow a risk-sensitive model of capacity determination? An experimental video survey. *Psychosomatics, 47,* 325–329.

Kim, S. Y. H., Cox, C., & Caine, E. D. (2002a). Impaired decision-making ability and willingness to participate in research in persons with Alzheimer's disease. *American Journal of Psychiatry, 159,* 797–802.

Kim, S. Y. H., Karlawish, J. H. T., & Caine, E. D. (2002b). Current state of research on decision-making competence of cognitively impaired elderly persons. *American Journal of Geriatric Psychiatry, 10,* 151–165.

Knowles, F. E., Liberto, J., Baker, F. M., Ruskin, P. E., & Raskin, A. (1994). Competency evaluations in a VA hospital. A 10-year perspective. *General Hospital Psychiatry, 16,* 119–124.

Krynski, M. D., Tymchuk, A. J., & Ouslander, J. G. (1994). How informed can consent be? New light on comprehension among elderly people making decisions about enteral tube feeding. *Gerontologist, 34,* 36–43.

Lapid, M. I., Rummans, T. A., Poole, K. L., Pankratz, S., Maurer, M. S., Rasmussen, K. G., et al. (2003). Decisional capacity of severely depressed patients requiring electroconvulsive therapy. *Journal of ECT, 19,* 67–72.

Lidz, C. W., & Appelbaum, P. S. (2002). The therapeutic misconception: Problems and solutions. *Medical Care, 49,* V55–V63.

Lombardo, P. (2008). *Three generations, no imbeciles: Eugenics, the Supreme Court, and Buck v. Bell.* Baltimore, MD: Johns Hopkins University Press.

Luce, J. M., & White, D. B. (2007). The pressure to withhold or withdraw life-sustaining therapy from critically ill patients in the United States. *American Journal of Respiratory and Critical Care Medicine, 175,* 1104–1108.

Manson, N., & O'Neill, O. (2007). *Rethinking informed consent in bioethics.* New York: Cambridge University Press.

Markson, L. J., Kern, D. C., Annas, G. J., & Glantz, L. H. (1994). Physician assessment of patient competence. *Journal of the American Geriatrics Society, 42,* 1074–1080.

Marson, D. C., Annis, S. M., McInturff, B., Bartolucci, A., & Harrell, L. E. (1999). Error behaviors associated with loss of competency in Alzheimer's disease. *Neurology, 53,* 1983–1992.

Marson, D. C., Chatterjee, A., Ingram, K. K., & Harrell, L. E. (1996). Toward a neurologic model of competency: Cognitive predictors of capacity to consent in Alzheimer's disease using three different legal standards. *Neurology, 46,* 666–672.

Marson, D. C., Cody, H. A., Ingram, K. K., & Harrell, L. E. (1995a). Neuropsychological predictors of competency in Alzheimer's disease using a rational reasons legal standard. *Archives of Neurology, 52,* 955–959.

Marson, D. C., Dreer, L. E., Krzywanski, S., Huthwaite, J. S., Devivo, M. J., & Novack, T. A. (2005). Impairment and partial recovery of medical decision-making capacity in traumatic brain injury: A 6-month longitudinal study. *Archives of Physical Medicine Rehabilitation, 86,* 889–895.

Marson, D. C., Earnst, K., Jamil, F., Bartolucci, A., & Harrell, L. (2000). Consistency of physicians' legal standard and personal judgments of competency in patients with Alzheimer's disease. *Journal of the American Geriatrics Society, 48,* 911–918.

Marson, D. C., Hawkins, L., McInturff, B., & Harrell, L. E. (1997). Cognitive models that predict physician judgments of capacity to consent in mild Alzheimer's disease. *Journal of the American Geriatrics Society, 45,* 458–464.

Marson, D. C., Ingram, K. K., Cody, H. A., & Harrell, L. E. (1995b). Assessing the competency of patients with Alzheimer's disease under different legal standards. A prototype instrument. *Archives of Neurology, 52,* 949–954.

Marson, D. C., McInturff, B., Hawkins, L., Bartolucci, A., & Harrell, L. E. (1997). Consistency of physician judgments of capacity to consent in mild Alzheimer's disease. *Journal of the American Geriatrics Society, 45,* 453–457.

Maryland (2007). Maryland Health—General Code Annotated. 5–603 (2005, 2007 Supp.)

Masand, P. S., Bouckoms, A. J., Fischel, S. V., Calabrese, L. V., & Stern, T. A. (1998). A prospective multicenter study of competency evaluations by psychiatric consultation services. *Psychosomatics, 39*, 55–60.

Mayberg, H., Lozano, A., Voon, V., McNeely, H., Seminowicz, D., Hamani, C., et al. (2005). Deep brain stimulation for treatment-resistant depression. *Neuron, 45*, 651–660.

McKegney, F. P., Schwartz, B. J., & O'Dowd, M. A. (1992). Reducing unnecessary psychiatric consultations for informed consent by liaison with administration. *General Hospital Psychiatry, 14*, 15–19.

Meagher, D. J., Moran, M., Raju, B., Gibbons, D., Donnelly, S., Saunders, J., et al. (2007). Phenomenology of delirium: Assessment of 100 adult cases using standardised measures. *The British Journal of Psychiatry, 190*, 135–141.

Mebane, A. H., & Rauch, H. B. (1990). When do physicians request competency evaluations? *Psychosomatics, 31*, 40–46.

Meisel, A. (1998). Legal aspects of end-of-life decision making. In M. D. Steinberg & S. J. Youngner (Eds.). *End-of-life decisions: A psychosocial perspective* (pp. 235–258). Washington, DC: American Psychiatric Press, Inc.

Miller, C. K., O'Donnell, D. C., Searight, H. R., & Barbarash, R. A. (1996). The Deaconess Informed Consent Comprehension Test: An assessment tool for clinical research subjects. *Pharmacotherapy, 16*, 872–878.

Misra, S., Socherman, R., Park, B. S., Hauser, P., & Ganzini, L. (2008). Influence of mood state on capacity to consent to research in patients with bipolar disorder. *Bipolar Disorders, 10*, 303–309.

Mittal, D., Palmer, B. W., Dunn, L. B., Landes, R., Ghormley, C., Beck, C., et al. (2007). Comparison of two enhanced consent procedures for patients with mild Alzheimer disease or mild cognitive impairment. *The American Journal of Geriatric Psychiatry, 15*, 163–167.

Moser, D. J., Reese, R. L., Hey, C. T., Schultz, S. K., Arndt, S., Beglinger, L. J., et al. (2005). Using a brief intervention to improve decisional capacity in schizophrenia research. *Schizophrenia Bulletin, 32*, 116–120.

Moser, D. J., Schultz, S. K., Arndt, S., Benjamin, M. L., Fleming, F. W., Brems, C. S., et al. (2002). Capacity to provide informed consent for participation in schizophrenia and HIV research. *American Journal of Psychiatry, 159*, 1201–1207.

Moye, J. (2003). Competence to consent to treatment. In T. Grisso (Ed.), *Evaluating competencies: Forensic assessments and instruments* (2nd ed., pp. 391–458). New York: Kluwer Academic/Plenum Publishers.

Moye, J., & Marson, D. C. (2007). Assessment of decision-making capacity in older adults: An emerging area of practice and research. *The Journals of Gerontology. Series B, Psychological Sciences and Social Sciences, 62*, 3–11.

Mukherjee, D., & McDonough, C. (2006). Clinician perspectives on decision-making capacity after acquired brain injury. (Ethics in Practice). *Topics in Stroke Rehabilitation, 13*, 75.

Munetz, M., & Roth, L. H. (1985). Informing patients about tardive dyskinesia. *Archives of General Psychiatry, 42*, 866–871.

Myers, B., & Barrett, C. L. (1986). Competency issues in referrals to a consultation-liaison service. *Psychosomatics, 27*, 782–789.

National Bioethics Advisory Commission. (1998). *Research involving persons with mental disorders that may affect decisionmaking capacity* (Vol. 1). Rockville, MD: National Bioethics Advisory Commission.

National Center for Injury Prevention and Control. (2009). Retrieved February 25, 2009, from http://www.cdc.gov/TraumaticInjury/overview.html

The Nuremberg Code (1947). (1998). In A. R. Jonsen, R. M. Veatch, & L. Walters (Eds.). *Source book in bioethics: A documentary history* (pp. 11–12). Washington, DC: Georgetown University Press.

Nolan, M. T., Hughes, M., Narendra, D. P., Sood, J. R., Terry, P. B., Astrow, A. B., et al. (2005). When patients lack capacity: The roles that patients with terminal diagnoses would choose for their physicians and loved ones in making medical decisions. *Journal of Pain and Symptom Management, 30*, 342–353.

Okai, D., Owen, G., McGuire, H., Singh, S., Churchill, R., & Hotopf, M. (2007). Mental capacity in psychiatric patients: Systematic review. *The British Journal of Psychiatry, 191*, 291–297.

Okonkwo, O., Griffith, H. R., Belue, K., Lanza, S., Zamrini, E. Y., Harrell, L. E., et al. (2007). Medical decision-making capacity in patients with mild cognitive impairment. *Neurology, 69*, 1528–1535.

Owen, G. S., Cutting, J., & David, A. (2007). Are people with schizophrenia more logical than healthy volunteers? *The British Journal of Psychiatry, 191*, 453–454.

Owen, G., Richardson, G., David, A. S., Szmukler, G., Hayward, P., & Hotopf, M. (2008). Mental capacity to make decisions on treatment in people admitted to psychiatric hospitals: Cross sectional study. *British Medical Journal, 337*, a448.

Palmer, B. W., Dunn, L. B., Appelbaum, P. S., & Jeste, D. V. (2004). Correlates of treatment-related decision-making capacity among middle-aged and older patients with schizophrenia. *Archives of General Psychiatry, 61*, 230–236.

Palmer, B. W., Dunn, L. B., Appelbaum, P. S., Mudaliar, S., Thal, L., Henry, R., et al. (2005). Assessment of capacity to consent to research among older persons with schizophrenia, Alzheimer disease, or diabetes mellitus: Comparison of a 3-item questionnaire with a comprehensive standardized capacity instrument. *Archives of General Psychiatry, 62,* 726–733.

Palmer, B. W., & Savla, G. N. (2007). The association of specific neuropsychological deficits with capacity to consent to research or treatment. *Journal of the International Neuropsychological Society, 13,* 1047–1059.

Plassman, B. L., Langa, K. M., Fisher, G. G., Heeringa, S. G., Weir, D. R., Ofstedal, M. B., et al. (2007). Prevalence of dementia in the United States: The aging, demographics, and memory study. *Neuroepidemiology, 29,* 125–132.

Plassman, B. L., Langa, K. M., Fisher, G. G., Heeringa, S. G., Weir, D. R., Ofstedal, M. B., et al. (2008). Prevalence of cognitive impairment without dementia in the United States. *Annals of Internal Medicine, 148,* 427–434.

Prendergast, T. J., Claessens, M. T., & Luce, J. M. (1998). A national survey of end-of-life care for critically ill patients. *American Journal of Respiratory and Critical Care Medicine, 158,* 1163–1167.

Prentice, K. J., Appelbaum, P. S., Conley, R. R., & Carpenter, W. T. (2007). Maintaining informed consent validity during lengthy research protocols. *IRB, 29,* 1–6.

President's Commission for the Study of Ethical Problems in Medicine and Biomedical and Behavioral Research. (1982). *Making health care decisions: The ethical and legal implications of informed consent in the patient–practitioner relationship (Vol. 1: Report).* Washington, DC: President's Commission for the Study of Ethical Problems in Medicine and Biomedical and Behavioral Research.

Pruchno, R. A., Smyer, M. A., Rose, M. S., Hartman-Stein, P. E., & Henderson-Laribee, D. L. (1995). Competence of long-term care residents to participate in decisions about their medical care: A brief, objective assessment. *Gerontologist, 35,* 622–629.

Ranjith, G., & Hotopf, M. (2004). Refusing treatment—Please see: An analysis of capacity assessments carried out by a liaison psychiatry service. *Journal of the Royal Society of Medicine, 97,* 480–482.

Raymont, V., Bingley, W., Buchanan, A., David, A. S., Hayward, P., Wessely, S., et al. (2004). Prevalence of mental incapacity in medical inpatients and associated risk factors: Cross-sectional study. *The Lancet, 364,* 1421–1427.

Reid-Proctor, G. M., Galin, K., & Cumming, M. A. (2001). Evaluation of legal competency in patients with frontal lobe injury. *Brain Injury, 15,* 377–386.

Reilly, P. (1991). *The surgical solution: A history of involuntary sterilization in the United States.* Baltimore, MD: Johns Hopkins University Press.

Rikkert, M. G., van den Bercken, J. H., ten Have, H. A., & Hoefnagels, W. H. (1997). Experienced consent in geriatrics research: A new method to optimize the capacity to consent in frail elderly subjects. *Journal of Medical Ethics, 23,* 271–276.

Rosen, M. I., & Rosenheck, R. (1999). Substance use and assignment of representative payees. *Psychiatric Services, 50,* 95–98.

Roth, L. H., Lidz, C. W., Meisel, A., Soloff, P. H., Kaufman, K., Spiker, D. G., et al. (1982). Competency to decide about treatment or research: An overview of some empirical data. *International Journal of Law and Psychiatry, 5,* 29–50.

Roth, L. H., Meisel, A., & Lidz, C. W. (1977). Tests of competency to consent to treatment. *American Journal of Psychiatry, 134,* 279–284.

Royall, D. R. (1994). Precis of executive dyscontrol as a cause of problem behavior in dementia. *Experimental Aging Research, 20,* 73–94.

Royall, D. R., Cordes, J., & Polk, M. (1997). Executive control and the comprehension of medical information by elderly retirees. *Experimental Aging Research, 23,* 301–313.

Royall, D. R., & Mahurin, R. (1994). EXIT, QED, and DSM-IV: Very early Alzheimer's disease. *Journal of Neuropsychiatry, 6,* 62–65.

Royall, D. R., Mahurin, R. K., & Gray, K. F. (1992). Bedside assessment of executive cognitive impairment: The executive interview. *Journal of the American Geriatrics Society, 40,* 1221–1226.

Sachs, G. A., Stocking, C. B., Stern, R., Cox, D. M., Hougham, G., & Sachs, R. S. (1994). Ethical aspects of dementia research: Informed consent and proxy consent. *Clinical Research, 42,* 403–412.

Saks, E., Dunn, L., Marshall, B., Navak, G., Golshan, S., & Jeste, D. V. (2002). The California Scale of Appreciation: A new instrument to measure the appreciation component of capacity to consent to research. *American Journal of Geriatric Psychiatry, 10,* 166–174.

Saks, E., Dunn, L., Wimer, J., Gonzales, M., & Kim, S. (2008). Proxy consent to research: Legal landscape. *Yale Journal of Health Law, Policy, and Ethics, 8,* 37–78.

Sass, H. (1983). Reichsrundschreiben 1931: Pre-Nuremberg German regulations concerning new therapy and human experimentation. *Journal of Medicine and Philosophy, 8,* 99–111.

Schachter, D., Kleinman, I., Prendergast, P., Remington, G., & Schertzer, S. (1994). The effect of psychopathology on the ability of schizophrenic patients to give informed consent. *Journal of Nervous and Mental Disorders, 182,* 360–362.

Schindler, B. A., Ramchandani, D., Matthews, M. K., & Podell, K. (1995). Competency and the frontal lobe. The impact of executive dysfunction on decisional capacity. *Psychosomatics, 36,* 400–404.

Schmand, B., Gouwenberg, B., Smit, J. H., & Jonker, C. (1999). Assessment of mental competency in community-dwelling elderly. *Alzheimer Disease and Associated Disorders, 13*, 80–87.

Schneider, C. (1998). *The practice of autonomy.* New York: Oxford.

Schneiderman, L. J., Jecker, N. S., & Jonsen, A. R. (1990). Medical futility: Its meaning and ethical implications. *Annals of Internal Medicine, 112*, 949–954.

Sehgal, A., Galbraith, A., Chesney, M., Schoenfeld, P., Charles, G., & Lo, B. (1992). How strictly do dialysis patients want their advance directive followed? *Journal of American Medical Association, 267*, 59–63.

Shalowitz, D. I., Garrett-Mayer, E., & Wendler, D. (2006). The accuracy of surrogate decision makers: A systematic review. *Archives of Internal Medicine, 166*, 493–497.

Silveira, M. J., Kim, S. Y. H., & Langa, K. M. (2009, February). Do living wills work in practice? Abstract presented at the 2009 VA HSRD Annual Meeting, Baltimore MD.

Silverman, H. J., Luce, J. M., & Schwartz, J. (2004). Protecting subjects with decisional impairment in research: The need for a multifaceted approach. *American Journal of Respiratory and Critical Care Medicine, 169*, 10–14.

Sprung, C. L., Cohen, S. L., Sjokvist, P., Baras, M., Bulow, H. H., Hovilehto, S., et al. (2003). End-of-life practices in European intensive care units: The Ethicus study. *Journal of the American Medical Association, 290*, 790–797.

Srebnik, D., Appelbaum, P. S., & Russo, J. (2004). Assessing competence to complete psychiatric advance directives with the CAT-PAD. *Comprehensive Psychiatry, 45*, 239–245.

Stanley, B., Guido, J., Stanley, M., & Shortell, D. (1984). The elderly patient and informed consent. Empirical findings. *Journal of the American Medical Association, 252*, 1302–1306.

Stanley, B., Stanley, M., Guido, J., & Garvin, L. (1988). The functional competency of elderly at risk. *Gerontologist, 28*, 53–58.

Stiles, P. G., Poythress, N. G., Hall, A., Falkenbach, D., & Williams, R. (2001). Improving understanding of research consent disclosures among persons with mental illness. *Psychiatric Services, 52*, 780–785.

Stroup, S., & Appelbaum, P. S. (2003). The subject advocate: Protecting the interests of participants with fluctuating decisionmaking capacity. *IRB Ethics and Human Research, 25*, 9–11.

Stroup, S., Appelbaum, P., Swartz, M., Patel, M., Davis, S., Jeste, D., et al. (2005). Decision-making capacity for research participation among individuals in the CATIE schizophrenia trial. *Schizophrenia Research, 80*, 1–8.

Studdert, D. M., Mello, M. M., Levy, M. K., Gruen, R. L., Dunn, E. J., Orav, E. J., et al. (2007). Geographic variation in informed consent law: Two standards for disclosure of treatment risks. *Journal of Empirical Legal Studies, 4,* 103–124.

Sturman, E. D. (2005). The capacity to consent to treatment and research: A review of standardized assessment tools. *Clinical Psychology Review, 25,* 954–974.

Sulmasy, D. P., Hughes, M. T., Thompson, R. E., Astrow, A. B., Terry, P. B., Kub, J., et al. (2007). How would terminally ill patients have others make decisions for them in the event of decisional incapacity? A longitudinal study. *Journal of the American Geriatrics Society, 55,* 1981–1988.

Swanson, J. W., McCrary, S. V., Swartz, M. S., Elbogen, E. B., & Van Dorn, R. A. (2006a). Superseding psychiatric advance directives: Ethical and legal considerations. *Journal of the American Academy of Psychiatry and the Law, 34,* 385–394.

Swanson, J. W., Swartz, M. S., Elbogen, E. B., Van Dorn, R. A., Ferron, J., Wagner, H. R., et al. (2006b). Facilitated psychiatric advance directives: A randomized trial of an intervention to foster advance treatment planning among persons with severe mental illness. *American Journal of Psychiatry, 163,* 1943–1951.

Tan, J. O. A., Stewart, A., Fitzpatrick, R., & Hope, T. (2006). Competence to make treatment decisions in Anorexia Nervosa: Thinking processes and values. *Philosophy, Psychiatry, Psychology, 13,* 267–282.

Taub, H. A., & Baker, M. T. (1983). The effect of repeated testing upon comprehension of informed consent materials by elderly volunteers. *Experimental Aging Research, 9,* 135–138.

Taub, H. A., Kline, G. E., & Baker, M. T. (1981). The elderly and informed consent: Effects of vocabulary level and corrected feedback. *Experimental Aging Research, 7,* 137–146.

Tymchuk, A. J., Ouslander, J. G., & Rader, N. (1986). Informing the elderly. A comparison of four methods. *Journal of the American Geriatrics Society, 34,* 818–822.

Umapathy, C., Ramchandani, D., Lamdan, R. M., Kishel, L. A., & Schindler, B. A. (1999). Competency evaluations on the consultation-liaison service: Some overt and covert aspects. *Psychosomatics, 40,* 28–33.

Valenstein, E. S. (1986). *Great and desperate cures: The rise and decline of psychosurgery and other radical treatments for mental illness.* New York: Basic Books.

Vellinga, A., Smit, J. H., van Leeuwen, E., van Tilburg, W., & Jonker, C. (2004). Competence to consent to treatment of geriatric patients: Judgements of physicians, family members, and the vignette method. *International Journal of Geriatric Psychiatry, 19,* 645–654.

Volicer, L., & Ganzini, L. (2003). Health professionals' views on standards for decision-making capacity regarding refusal of medical treatment in mild Alzheimer's disease. *Journal of the American Geriatrics Society, 51,* 1270–1274.

Vollmann, J., Bauer, A., Danker-Hopfe, H., & Helmchen, H. (2003). Competence of mentally ill patients: A comparative empirical study. *Psychological Medicine, 33,* 1463–1471.

Vollmann, J., & Winau, R. (1996). The Prussian regulation of 1900: Early ethical standards for human experimentation in Germany. *IRB, 18,* 9–11.

Wendler, D., & Prasad, K. (2001). Core safeguards for clinical research with adults who are unable to consent. *Annals of Internal Medicine, 135,* 514–523.

Wendler, D., & Rackoff, J. (2002). Consent for continuing research participation: What is it and when should it be obtained? *IRB, 24,* 1–6.

Wenger, N. S., & Halpern, J. (1994). Can a patient refuse a psychiatric consultation to evaluate decision-making capacity? *Journal of Clinical Ethics, 5,* 230–234.

White, D. B., Curtis, J. R., Wolf, L. E., Prendergast, T. J., Taichman, D. B., Kuniyoshi, G., et al. (2007). Life support for patients without a surrogate decision maker: Who decides? *Annals of Internal Medicine, 147,* 34–40.

Whyte, S., Jacoby, R., & Hope, T. (2004). Testing doctors' ability to assess patients' competence. *International Journal of Law and Psychiatry, 27,* 291–298.

Wicclair, M. (1991). Patient decision-making capacity and risk. *Bioethics, 5,* 91–104.

Wilder, C. M., Elbogen, E. B., Swartz, M. S., Swanson, J. W., & Van Dorn, R. A. (2007). Effect of patients' reasons for refusing treatment on implementing psychiatric advance directives. *Psychiatric Services, 58,* 1348–1350.

Wirshing, D. A., Wirshing, W. C., Marder, S. R., Liberman, R. P., & Mintz, J. (1998). Informed consent: Assessment of comprehension. *American Journal of Psychiatry, 155,* 1508–1511.

Wittink, M. N., Morales, K. H., Meoni, L. A., Ford, D. E., Wang, N. Y., Klag, M. J., et al. (2008). Stability of preferences for end-of-life treatment after 3 years of follow-up: The Johns Hopkins Precursors Study. *Archives of Internal Medicine, 168,* 2125–2130.

Wong, J., Clare, I., Holland, A., Watson, P., & Gunn, M. (2000). The capacity of people with a "mental disability" to make a health care decision. *Psychological Medicine, 30,* 295–306.

World Health Organization. (2005). *WHO resource book on mental health, human rights and legislation.* Geneva: World Health Organization.

Youngner, S. J. (1998). Competence to refuse life-sustaining treatment. In S. J. Youngner & M. D. Steinberg (Eds.). *End-of-life decisions: A psychosocial perspective* (pp. 19–54). Washington, DC: American Psychiatric Press.

Cases and Statutes

Arizona Rev. Stat. Title 36-3231 (2003).

California Health and Safety Code, Amendment to § 24178 (2002).

Canterbury v. Spence, 464 F.2d 772 (1972).

Cobbs v. Grant, 8 Cal. 3d 229 (1972).

Code of Virginia, Title 32.1, § 162.16–162.18.

Cruzan v. Director, Missouri Department of Health, 497 U.S. 261 (1990).

Illinois Health Care Surrogate Act, 755 ILCS 40/10 (2007).

In re Conroy, Supreme Court of NJ 1984; 98 NJ 321, 486 A2d 1209 (1984).

Maryland, Md Health-Gen. Code Ann. § 5–603 (2005, Supp. 2007).

Mental Capacity Act of England and Wales (2005).

Natanson v. Kline, 350 P2d 1093 (1960).

New Jersey, Access to Medical Research Act. 26, 14.1–14.5 (2008).

New York State Public Health Law Article 29-B, 2960–2979, Orders Not to Resuscitate (1987).

New York State Public Health Law Article 29-C, 2980–2994, Health Care Agents and Proxies (1990).

Oregon Health Care Decisions Act (1977, 1983, 1987, 1993), Or. Rev. Stat. §§ 127.505 to 127.642.

Rennie v. Klein, 462 F. Supp. 1131 (1978).

Rivers v. Katz, 495 N.E.2d 337, 343 (1986).

Rogers v. Okin, 478 F. Supp. 1342 (1979).

Salgo v. Leland Stanford Jr., University Board of Trustees, 317 P.2d 170 (1957).

Schloendorff v. Society of New York Hospital, 211 N.Y. 125, 105 N.E. 92 (1914).

Slater v. Baker and Stapleton, 95 Eng Rep 860 (1767).

Key Words

advance directive: sometimes called advance medical directive, advance health care directive, etc.; usually refers to a written directive about medical decision making for a patient in case of his future incapacity.

appreciation standard: the ability to apply the medical and personal facts to one's own situation, and by implication requires the ability to form adequate beliefs about those facts.

authenticity criterion: often proposed philosophical criterion for capacity that emphasizes the ability to make a decision based on one's own values.

best interests standard: standard in which the surrogate or proxy attempts to weigh the burdens and the benefits of various options, and chooses the one that has the best benefit-to-burden profile.

capacity: more commonly referred to as "decision-making capacity" in most modern laws, it refers to the functional status of a patient to provide independent informed consent to a medical procedure or treatment.

competence: synonymous with capacity, except when used specifically to refer to adjudicated competence or capacity of a patient, in which case it should be referred to as "adjudicated competence (or capacity)."

evidencing a choice standard: the standard of being able to communicate a choice; a low-level, necessary condition but not sufficient to consider someone competent.

executive functions: a loosely defined collection of cognitive brain processes (e.g., planning, abstract thinking, initiation, and inhibition) that manages or coordinates other lower-level cognitive processes.

functionalist model of competence: competence is not determined by a status (e.g., age) or diagnosis or a label, but rather the actual performance required for the task in question.

informed consent: consent requirement based on the right to self-determination that emphasizes autonomous decision making by the patient; it requires a *competent* person making a voluntary choice after receiving *adequate information*.

institutional review board (IRB): sometimes called research ethics committee (REC) or research ethics board (REB) depending on the jurisdiction, it is the committee that reviews human subjects' research protocols to ensure compliance with ethical principles embodied in a jurisdiction's regulations.

instructional health care directive: also called a living will, the directive provides advance preferences or instructions for anticipated future medical scenarios in which the patient becomes incompetent.

legally authorized representative (LAR): strictly speaking, this is a legal term defined by the Federal regulations, referring to persons who may give legal permission for another, incompetent person to be enrolled in research. However, the actual content of this term is, per Federal regulations, decided by the states or local government. Few states have clear laws defining LAR.

objective patient-centered standard: sometimes also called the reasonable persons standard, the "patient" in a patient-centered disclosure standard is not some specific individual but a legal construct of a "reasonable" person or a "typical" person.

patient-centered standards of disclosure: the nature and extent of the required disclosures for informed consent are determined by the needs of the patient; this has two versions, an objective and a subjective standard (see below).

presumption of capacity: the default assumption about an adult; challenging this presumption (i.e., having a reason to specifically evaluate capacity) is distinct from determining the lack of it.

professional standards of disclosure: the nature and extent of the required disclosures for informed consent are determined by what a reasonable physician would disclose to a similarly situated patient.

proxy advance directive: an advance directive that designates a surrogate or proxy decision maker in case the patient becomes incompetent.

reasoning standard: a variety of "reasoning" processes, such as comparing, inferring, and balancing information in the process of arriving at a decision, rather than on the reasonableness of the content of the preference.

risk–benefit context or profile: the main contextual factor to incorporate into the process of translating an assessment of a patient's abilities into a categorical judgment about that patient's capacity status; in general, the lower the risk and the greater the benefit, the lower the level of abilities needed to be deemed competent, and vice versa.

simple consent: consent requirement based on the right to be free from unwanted intrusion, in contrast to informed consent, which is based on the right to make an informed, autonomous decision.

subjective patient-centered standard: the "patient" in the patient-centered disclosure standard is the particular patient in question rather than some abstract, fictional person; thus, the required elements of disclosures are those items that the particular patient needs to make an informed decision.

substituted judgment standard: standard of decision making for an incompetent patient in which the surrogate or proxy attempts to choose what the patient, were she currently competent, would choose.

surrogate decision maker: when a patient is deemed incompetent, the person who makes decisions in the patient's place; in this book, used interchangeably with "proxy" decision maker.

understanding standard: the ability to understand the relevant medical facts, specifically referring to the intellectual comprehension of those facts rather than beliefs concerning them.

Index

About the Author

Scott Kim, MD, PhD, is an associate professor of psychiatry, a core faculty member of the Bioethics Program, and an investigator in the Center for Behavioral and Decision Sciences in Medicine at the University of Michigan. Prior to joining the University of Michigan faculty in 2004, he was the director of the Program in Clinical Ethics at the University of Rochester Medical Center where he also directed the Ethics Consultation Service. Dr. Kim's work combines his background in philosophy (PhD in ethical theory, University of Chicago), his experience as a consultant–liaison psychiatrist and as an ethics consultant, and his empirical research in bioethics. He has served as a consultant to a variety of organizations, including the American Psychiatric Association, American College of Neuropsychopharmacology, the Institute of Medicine, and the National Institute of Mental Health. He has published seminal empirical, theoretical, and methodological papers on the concept of decision-making capacity, the ethics of surrogate consent for research, and the ethics of informed consent for high risk research. He was awarded the Academy of Psychosomatic Medicine 2006 Dorfman Award for Best Article for Original Research. His research has been supported by the American Association for Geriatric Psychiatry and by several grants from the National Institutes of Health. He is currently a Greenwall Foundation Faculty Scholar in Bioethics.